JOSSEY-BASS

Test Talk!

Understanding the Stakes and Helping Your Children Do Their Best

Cheli Cerra, M.Ed. & Ruth Jacoby, Ed.D.

WILEY
1807
2007

John Wiley & Sons, Inc.

Copyright © 2007 by Cheli Cerra and Ruth Jacoby. All rights reserved.

Published by Jossey-Bass
A Wiley Imprint
989 Market Street, San Francisco, CA 94103-1741   www.josseybass.com

No part of this publication may be reproduced, stored in a retrieval system, or transmitted in any form or by any means, electronic, mechanical, photocopying, recording, scanning, or otherwise, except as permitted under Section 107 or 108 of the 1976 United States Copyright Act, without either the prior written permission of the publisher, or authorization through payment of the appropriate per-copy fee to the Copyright Clearance Center, Inc., 222 Rosewood Drive, Danvers, MA 01923, 978-750-8400, fax 978-646-8600, or on the Web at www.copyright.com. Requests to the publisher for permission should be addressed to the Permissions Department, John Wiley & Sons, Inc., 111 River Street, Hoboken, NJ 07030, 201-748-6011, fax 201-748-6008, or online at http://www.wiley.com/go/permissions.

Permission is given for individual classroom teachers to reproduce the pages and illustrations for classroom use. Reproduction of these materials for an entire school system is strictly forbidden.

Limit of Liability/Disclaimer of Warranty: While the publisher and author have used their best efforts in preparing this book, they make no representations or warranties with respect to the accuracy or completeness of the contents of this book and specifically disclaim any implied warranties of merchantability or fitness for a particular purpose. No warranty may be created or extended by sales representatives or written sales materials. The advice and strategies contained herein may not be suitable for your situation. You should consult with a professional where appropriate. Neither the publisher nor author shall be liable for any loss of profit or any other commercial damages, including but not limited to special, incidental, consequential, or other damages.

Jossey-Bass books and products are available through most bookstores. To contact Jossey-Bass directly call our Customer Care Department within the U.S. at 800-956-7739, outside the U.S. at 317-572-3986, or fax 317-572-4002.

Jossey-Bass also publishes its books in a variety of electronic formats. Some content that appears in print may not be available in electronic books.

ISBN: 978-0-7879-8274-4

Printed in the United States of America
FIRST EDITION
PB Printing   10 9 8 7 6 5 4 3 2 1

The Buzz About *Test Talk!*

"Many parents are frustrated that their children spend many hours studying, but they are not always getting the best results. Test Talk! will help students improve their self-confidence and feel that they will be test savvy with practice. The worksheets, checklists, and templates included will give parents tips and strategies to use to encourage better study habits."

Dr. Hui Fang Hwang "Angie" Su, *Professor of Mathematics Education for Nova Southeastern University and creator of Project MIND—Math Is Not Difficult*

"What a simple, practical guide to all the questions parents could possibly have about test taking and their child. Each scenario is on point and so is the answer to it! I can't wait to introduce this book to our parents in Las Vegas! They are eager to help their children succeed in ALL areas of academics! This will go a long way to helping them do just that!"

Vickie Frazier-Williams, *Vice President, Imagine Schools, and Former TV Personality*

"Test Talk! is a handy tool for parents and students alike. The tips and strategies presented can help students increase their test scores and reach a level of test confidence. Its easy-to-read format makes it a simple, fun way to gain effective tools for developing great study habits and test-taking skills."

Ana Del Cerro, *Public School Counselor*

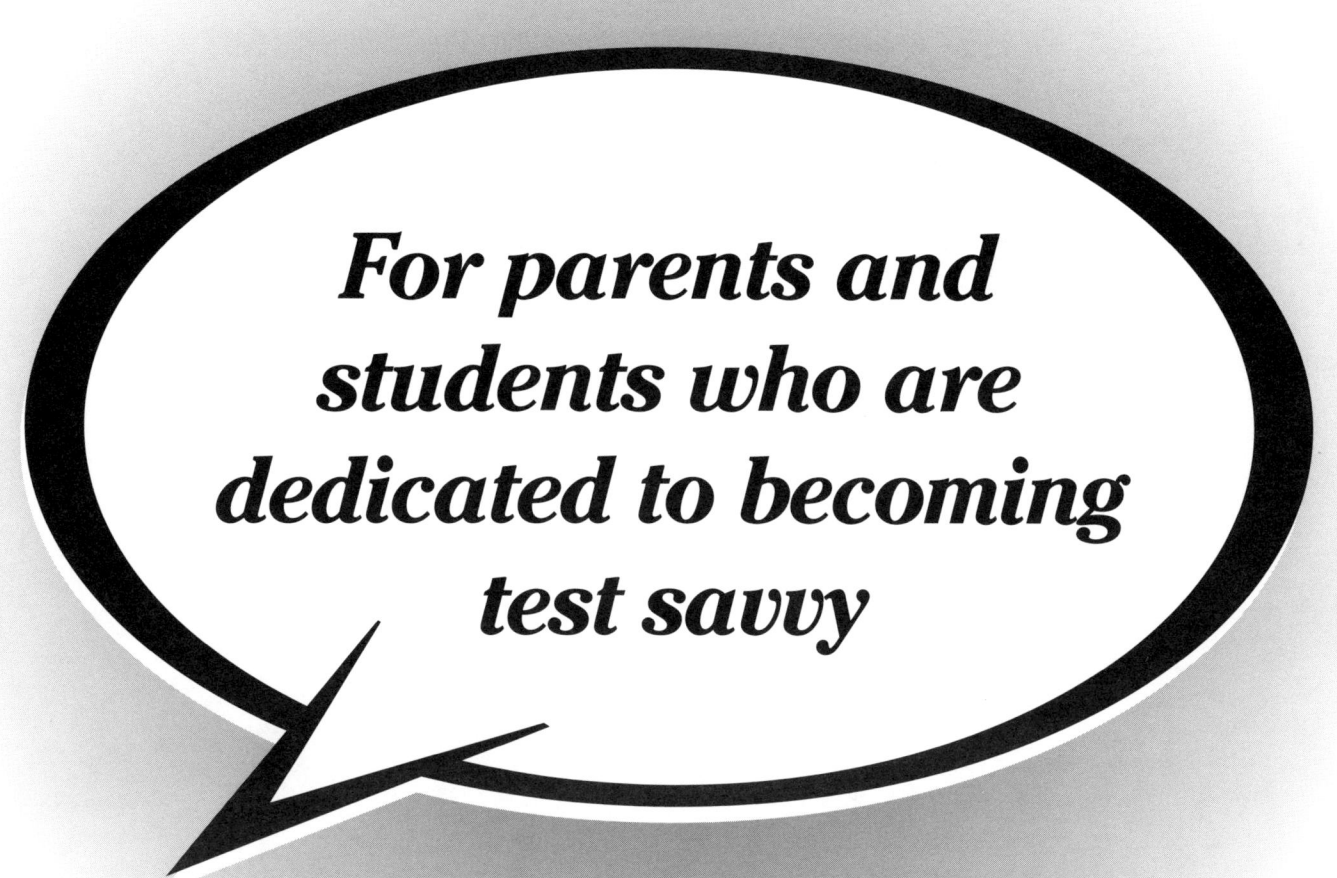

Table of Contents

Introduction: How to Use This Book ... ix
Chapter 1: Why Test? ... 1
Chapter 2: Savvy Study Skills ... 19
Chapter 3: No Test Stress! ... 47
Chapter 4: After the Test ... 65
Chapter 5: The Academic Portfolio ... 91
Appendix A: Glossary of Testing Terms ... 111
Appendix B: Resources and References ... 117
Answer Key ... 127
About the Authors ... 131

Introduction
HOW TO USE THIS BOOK

> "Always bear in mind that your own resolution to succeed is more important than any other one thing."
> **Abraham Lincoln**

Testing—a word that strikes fear into the hearts of students and their parents—is an undeniable part of academic life. For a teacher, a test can be a valuable tool for gauging a child's progress in school. Teachers can use testing to assess a student's strengths and weaknesses and identify both learning styles and learning problems. In addition, since the passage of the No Child Left Behind Act in 2002, states have been required to test students in all public schools in order to evaluate how well the schools are doing their job. Yet even though testing is just another way to evaluate learning, it can cause tremendous stress for many students. No child wants to fail a test, nor do parents want to see their child upset by the thought of an impending test or by a disappointing test score.

As a parent, you can help your child with testing by being informed about the tests your child will be taking, how the test results will affect him, and what you can do to reduce test stress and increase academic achievement. Our goal in writing this book is to show you how to become "test savvy" by helping you grasp the who, what, when, and why of tests.

The book is divided into five chapters, each focusing on an important aspect of testing. We begin by introducing the reasons for testing and continue with study skills, tips for stressless testing, and information on what to do after the test. The final chapter will show you how to create an academic portfolio, in which you can keep all the information you need, organized in an easy-to-read format, to track the progress of your child.

Snapshots throughout the book provide examples of real-life situations parents face when dealing with both their children and the school—on tests and testing results. Each snapshot is followed by strategies and tips for eliminating the potential problems that come with testing. Worksheets, checklists, sample letters, and contracts provided throughout the book are designed to support you in helping your child get organized and become skilled at applying acquired knowledge in any test format. Sidebars will give you additional points on what you can do to ensure test success by presenting a specific problem and a workable solution. At the end of each chapter we've added a "Make It Happen Test" that focuses on the key points offered in the chapter. If you use these tools, you can be assured that your child will know how to review and study for tests, work independently, manage study time well, and consistently test with greater confidence and success.

Our ultimate goal is to give your child the know-how to achieve positive results on tests of all types: teacher-made tests, end-of-level book exams, midterms and finals, quizzes, and mandatory state and district exams, including those all-important standardized achievement tests.

You play a big part in your child's success. To better understand testing, be sure to look at both Appendix A, which offers a glossary of testing terms, and Appendix B, which gives resources and references that will allow you to find out about all the exams, including those at the state and district levels, that your child will need to take.

With this book, you will be:

- *Pr*oactive: Become a take-charge parent and a can-doer, working in your child's best interest. Seek assistance and advice from the school as soon as problems arise with grades and test results. Don't wait!
- *O*rganized: Help your child set up a test study schedule and stick to it. Use the strategies and test studying contracts in this book to assist your child with her studying responsibilities. Be ready to celebrate the successes and conquer the challenges.
- *W*ell-prepared: Set up an environment at home that shows your child that studying and reviewing each night is a top priority if he is going to succeed in school. Set an example by asking about class work and working with your child on reexamining work done in class and homework from previous nights. Decrease television, computer, and telephone usage, and quiz your child for a few minutes each night on a specific subject, especially if you know he is weak in that subject and a test is coming up.
- *E*ffective: Know that communication is key. First, make sure that the school is explaining the nature of upcoming tests to your child, and that you understand what they're all about as well. Don't be afraid to ask questions, and be prepared to telephone, write notes, or e-mail the school, especially as soon as any problems arise. Waiting can jeopardize your child's progress. Second, be ready to communicate the plans you have laid out to your child and remind him that the more he reviews and studies, and the more he focuses in class and takes good notes, the better his school grades and scores on standardized tests will be.
- *R*eflective: Take the "Make It Happen Test" at the end of each chapter to help you review, reflect on, and plan winning strategies.

Now you have the POWER to create a smooth-running and hassle-free evening, where test preparation is effectively completed without complaints and reminders.

Five Steps to Test Success

Step 1: Test Communication Assessment

Take the following Test Communication Assessment. This will help you determine your level of comfort in speaking with school staff and with your child about studying and test grades.

Directions: Circle yes or no to give the answer you find most appropriate. Count up the number of yes answers and then find the corresponding comments. Review the statements to which you answered no and keep them as your top priorities for improvement. Then move on to Step 2.

Yes No 1. I am comfortable speaking with teachers at conferences about my child's test results and grades.

Yes No 2. I listen more than I talk so I can learn how to get my child ready for test preparation and studying.

Yes No 3. I am comfortable requesting a conference with the teacher about test and studying issues.

Yes No 4. I am at ease when meeting with the school staff.

Yes No 5. I do not believe I know more than the teacher.

Yes No 6. I contact teachers immediately when my child has difficulty understanding material on an exam and/or has done poorly on a test.

Yes No 7. I like to have teacher talks.

Yes No 8. I speak to my child about school and ask what he learned that was new that day to demonstrate the importance of learning and reviewing information as a tool for test preparation.

Yes No 9. I respect the teacher's test policies and grading system.

Yes No 10. I have a studying policy for my child that stresses the importance of using a schedule and following rules for completing studying/reviewing successfully.

Tally the number of yes answers. If you scored:

8 or higher: You are on your way to becoming an effective communicator.

6 to 8: You may want to read carefully those snapshots addressing areas in which you are weak and practice the tips and techniques. The other snapshots may give you further insight and communication skills to improve your own conversational style and test-taking knowledge.

5 or below: You will want to read all the chapters and snapshots. Practice the tips and techniques, asking friends and family to assist you.

Step 2: Goals Assessment

Directions: Visualize your perfect night at home, where there are no complaints about homework, studying, and grades; everyone eats dinner at the same time; and there is even time for reading and leisure activities. Can this happen for your family? Yes, it can! Take a few minutes and follow these easy steps.

- Write down what it would take for things to go smoothly in your home each night. Be specific in your goals. Concentrate on your child's study and test preparation skills and how to incorporate these into a schedule.
- Rank each goal in order of importance.
- Read the snapshots detailed in the book that address those areas where you need assistance. Follow the ideas and put them into place.
- Make the goals a reality and they will be part of your nightly ritual. Studying and preparing for a test will no longer be a struggle, but an enriching and rewarding experience that will foster quality parent-child time and improve student achievement.

Step 3: Parent Homework Survey

To improve your understanding of your role in the test preparation process, fill out this survey and review the results. It will give you insight and help you help your child in her nightly study rituals.

Directions: Circle yes or no at the beginning of each statement to see how you view your role in the nightly studying process. Count up the number of yes answers and then find the corresponding comments, following.

Yes No 1. Do you inform the teacher immediately when your child does not understand the lessons on which he will be tested?

Yes No 2. Do you review with your child information she has studied?

Yes No 3. Are you assisting your child with studying as he needs it?

Yes No 4. Do you know when the teacher is giving a test?

Yes No 5. Do you have a study schedule and a study policy in your home?

Yes No 6. Do you have a quiet area in your home for doing homework?

Yes No 7. Do you reward test success?

Yes No 8. Does your child know that you feel studying and reviewing class work is a top priority?

Yes No 9. Do you have fellow classmates' phone numbers or the teacher's e-mail address in case your child forgets what he has to study?

Yes No 10. Are you conferencing with the teacher when you see grades dropping?

Yes No 11. Do you encourage your child to ask for assistance at home and at school?

Yes No 12. Do you give consequences when your child does not stick to her studying schedule, and are you consistent in giving those consequences?

Yes No 13. Do you have a set schedule for homework and studying for those days your child has no outside activities and an alternative schedule for those days your child has afterschool commitments?

Yes No 14. Do you conference with the teacher to come up with a plan to fix studying habits and grades? Do you follow up with the school? Do you carry out the plan?

Tally the yes answers. If you scored:

12 or higher: You have a handle on how to assist your child with studying habits.

9 to 11: You need to review some of your studying policies and make adjustments to increase your child's test success.

8 or below: Read the sections in the book that address how you can lend a hand in increasing your child's test accomplishments.

Step 4: Monthly Self-Evaluation

Use the following Monthly Self-Evaluation to help you keep on track. By reviewing and answering these questions each month, you will see where you need to make adjustments.

Directions: Answer these questions at the end of each month.

1. What are my child's studying struggles?
   _____
   _____
   _____

2. What are my child's studying successes?
   _____
   _____
   _____

3. What tip can I use to change a bad studying habit into an accomplishment?

   ❏ Create a schedule.
   ❏ Check my child's planner/journal (a notebook in which he writes down assignments, tests, project dates) nightly to see if any test dates are coming up.
   ❏ Assist with studying tips and review when needed.
   ❏ Give rewards for studying and test successes.
   ❏ Be consistent with consequences for a drop in grades or for not studying.
   ❏ Make studying a top priority.

   Other
   _____
   _____

4. How can I improve?
   _____
   _____
   _____

5. Am I asking the teacher for assistance?
   _____

6. Am I setting high expectations for my child?
   _____

7. Am I communicating to my child that reviewing and studying nightly will increase his grades and success on all tests?
   _____

8. Am I insisting that my child do her best at all times? _____

Step 5: Use This Book's Resources

Use Appendix B to locate references and resources your child can use to increase his skills and knowledge. You will also find sites that give information, state by state, on what is required to successfully pass specific tests.

Notes:

CHAPTER ONE
Why Test?

"The test of a good teacher is not how many questions he can ask his pupils that they will answer readily, but how many questions he inspires them to ask him which he finds it hard to answer."
Alice Wellington Rollins

What is the purpose of testing?
Contrary to what some students might think, giving a test is not a teacher's way of making their lives miserable. Tests offer many benefits in education, acting as checkpoints on the academic highway, and providing teachers and parents with valuable information. For example, a test might answer such questions as: Is a student's reading ability on grade level? Did a child understand the math chapter on decimals? Are there certain areas in which a student is weak? Testing is simply an efficient and effective method of measuring a student's progress.

Tests vary widely in how they are given and what they measure. Some are oral, others are written. Some tests are long, and others are short. Students can study for some tests by using specific material; other tests ask students to draw on the cumulative skills they've developed. Some tests are planned, whereas others are impromptu, such as the dreaded pop quiz. Knowing the reason for a test, the material it will cover, and what it takes for your child to pass successfully will assist you in helping your child prepare and succeed.

This chapter will address:

- Why students take tests
- The benefits of testing
- The different types of tests

The Snapshots:

1. What Is the Purpose of a State Achievement Test?
2. State Standards Are Confusing to Me and My Child
3. My Child Takes Too Many Tests and Doesn't Do Enough Reading
4. Why Give Take-Home Tests?
5. Why Must Special Education Students Go Through State Testing?
6. Are Final Exams Really Necessary?
7. My Daughter's Teacher Is Overtesting
8. Why Justify Test Answers?
9. Why Test at All?
10. Are Timed Tests Valid?
11. What Is the Purpose of a Writing Test?
12. How Can Essay Tests Be Graded?

www.school-talk.com

Snapshot #1: What Is the Purpose of a State Achievement Test?

My son is in third grade. I just received a letter from the school principal letting me know the students at my child's grade level will be given a state achievement test in two weeks. What is the purpose of testing children at such a young age? Is this necessary? What should I do?

Tip: Achievement tests fall under the category of *standardized tests*. Every state sets academic standards for what a child should know in each grade. A state achievement test measures how well your child is learning the standards for his grade. This test will examine what your child has learned up to this point in critical areas such as reading and math.

Your child's state assessment score or any other standardized score is only one source of information about your child's achievement. In effect, it provides a snapshot of your child—capturing a moment in your child's academic life. One test can't possibly give a complete view of your child's academic progress—but *you* can do that by creating an "academic portfolio." To learn how to do that, see Chapter Five.

In addition, the No Child Left Behind Act of 2001 (NCLB), which was signed into law on January 8, 2002, now affects every public school in America. This law reauthorizes a number of federal programs that seeks to improve performance of children in U.S. K–12 schools by increasing standards for states, school districts, and schools and at the same time providing parents more flexibility and choice. NCLB requires states to test all students in reading and math every year from grades 3 through 8 and then once again in high school to determine if the schools are making adequate yearly progress (AYP), based on state-determined criteria. In other words, the tests are designed to help states find out how good a job each school and school district is doing. For more information on NCLB, see Appendix B.

The first thing you can do to help your child prepare for a state achievement test is to alleviate his concerns about it. Talk with your child about what the test is all about and encourage him to do his best. Also, talk with the teacher about test-taking strategies your son can learn. In addition, many states have practice tests that can be downloaded from their Department of Education Web sites. (See Appendix B for a listing of these sites.) Have your son practice taking the test to become familiar with the testing format. Finally, show your support for your child by letting him know you are confident he will do his best.

Snapshot #2: State Standards Are Confusing to Me and My Child

All I keep hearing about are state standards and state standardized tests. It seems to me that teachers are very test- and skills-oriented. I am very confused about how this will improve my child's education. What should I do?

Topic: Standardized tests
Problem: Why do states put so much emphasis on standardized tests?
Solution: Understanding the importance of testing

Standardized tests are a way to outline the goals and objectives of a particular grade level. Whether the child is meeting these goals and objectives is measured by his performance on these state-mandated tests. Historically, such tests have been used to measure how students compare with each other (that is, they were norm-referenced) or how much of a particular curriculum they have learned (they were criterion-referenced). Nowadays, standardized tests are often used to make decisions about grade promotion or high school graduation. They also are intended to shape curriculum and instruction. When you receive the scores for the state assessment test, don't just look at the number of correct answers but also consider the breakdown of how well your child did in each area. These results will help you understand your child's strengths, weaknesses, and the skills he should have learned for his particular grade level.

Tip: Because of the federally mandated No Child Left Behind Act, standardized tests play a major role in your child's education. Several states also administer "high-stakes" tests that have an affect on class placement and grade promotion. Years ago, some states called these "minimum basic skills" tests. These standards are used as a yardstick against which to measure student performance. Teachers and school administrators use the results to help them shape curriculum and instruction, and to clarify student learning goals and learning gains. Many states' Department of Education Web sites have the standards for each grade level posted as well as practice tests that you can download. You may want to use these as a reference tool for working with your child at home. For further information, go to Appendix B and find your state's site for specific guidelines and testing information.

Snapshot #3: My Child Takes Too Many Tests and Doesn't Do Enough Reading

My daughter's school just got a new reading series. She is in fourth grade, and as part of this reading program she has to take several reading tests a week. I am upset that she is being tested so much. What should I do?

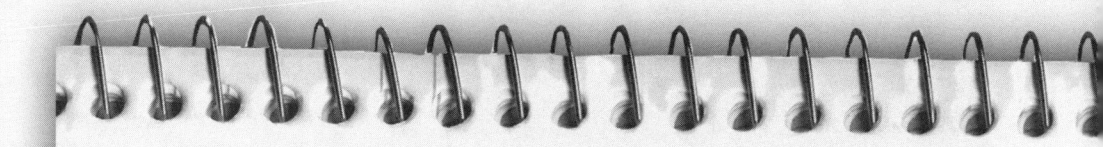

Tip: Many schools conduct specific reading tests to determine skills that might be lacking. In the primary grades, emphasis is given to phonemic awareness (understanding the sounds that letters make), fluency (the rate at which a child reads), and comprehension (understanding what is read). In the upper grades, critical literacy plays an important part in the reading program. Many children read without questioning what they are reading or understanding the author's point of view; critical literacy challenges students to think, analyze, and debate.

I would not be too concerned if these tests are done at the beginning of the year to determine the level at which your child reads. However, it is always important to know the reason why your child is tested. The best source for this information is your child's teacher. Schedule an appointment with the teacher and openly discuss your concerns. You may find that your child is doing very well, or alternatively, that your child needs help from you at home.

> *Assessments given early in the school year determine which skills have been mastered.*

Snapshot #4:
Why Give Take-Home Tests?

My son's fifth-grade science teacher gives him take-home tests. Because he is allowed to use the book to answer the questions, my son certainly isn't being tested on what he has learned. What is the point of such a test? Is the teacher just lazy? The idea of a take-home test seems utterly absurd, and I can't believe this is an effective way to test. What should I do?

Tip: Take-home tests are not that uncommon and can be given for a variety of reasons. Your child's teacher may plan to use the exact same test in the classroom at a later date to determine how much your child learned from the lesson. By allowing a child to take home a test and use the textbook, the teacher is promoting the development of certain skills, such as how to study independently, use a resource to find information, transfer and adapt what is in the book to answer a question on the test, and cultivate critical thinking skills. A take-home test offers an opportunity for your child to review the material, making sure he understood the lesson and did not miss anything important. And this type of review will show your child that he can use the same method to study for other subject areas.

Sit down with your child and ask him about the test. Chances are he needs to thoroughly research and read the sections in the chapter to provide answers to the questions. If you are still not convinced that take-home tests are right for your child, set up a meeting with the teacher to address this.

> *Take-home tests help a child discover independently important facts necessary to learning specific material. They also act as a review of the class lesson.*

Snapshot #5: Why Must Special Education Students Go Through State Testing?

My fifth-grade daughter has been placed in special education since first grade. Today she came home chanting: "I am ready, I am set, I will do well on the big test." When I asked her what she was talking about, she said that everyone in the school was getting ready to take a big test. I called the school and found out this test is the state's "high-stakes" test, which determines whether a child has successfully met the goals and objectives for the grade level. In some grades it determines promotion as well. I can't believe the test is taking place so early in the school year when the teacher has not finished covering the material in the textbook. I feel that because she has been a special education student since first grade, she should not be tested. What should I do?

> Be a proactive advocate for your child throughout the year, not just during times of testing.

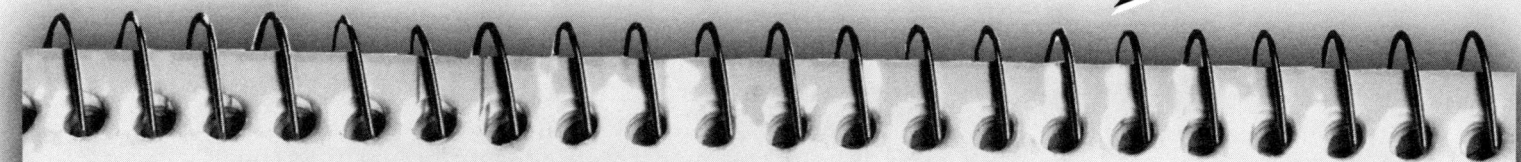

Tip: It is not unusual for children in your daughter's situation to be tested, and in fact, testing can be helpful to your daughter and the program she's in. Schools and school districts are accountable for the progress of all students—including those with special needs—and tests are a way of determining whether the schools have done their job. However, you want to be sure that the school is teaching your daughter the skills she needs to succeed, especially if she has to pass a high-stakes test for promotion. Your daughter's Individualized Education Plan (IEP) should explain whether she will participate in state- and district-wide assessments and if any accommodation will be given to her. Participation is determined by the IEP team, and you are part of this team. Call the school and schedule a meeting with the school counselor or assistant principal as soon as possible to discuss the reason for the test and the consequences for your child. Make sure you understand your child's rights under the Individuals with Disabilities Education Improvement Act of 2004 (IDEA). For information on the National Dissemination Center for Children with Disabilities, an important resource, see Appendix B.

Snapshot #6: Are Final Exams Really Necessary?

My son, who is in sixth grade, came home from school with the news that he will be having finals all next week. What is the purpose of a final exam when the teacher has been testing my son all through the school year? I don't see a point to giving a final exam, especially in each and every subject. What should I do?

Tip: Testing is part of the curriculum, especially when it comes to assessing whether your son has understood and mastered the grade-level goals, objectives, and expectations. These exams are important, because they highlight areas in which he may not understand certain material. If he has not mastered the grade-level standards, it will definitely make it harder for him to be successful as he moves into the next school year. If your son was not successfully learning the standard material in any of his subjects, his teacher should have already contacted you with her concerns.

It is also very important that your child learn how to study for final exams, especially in middle school. Your son's teacher will probably make study sheets and take-home study packets to help him prepare for the exams. If you want to help your son, you can also have him go through all of the chapter tests and quizzes that the teacher has given to date. This is a good way to review the material. Set up a study calendar, and you will see that your son will have a good experience with his final exams.

Test Talk! • Understanding the Stakes and Helping Your Children Do Their Best

Snapshot #7: My Daughter's Teacher Is Overtesting

My daughter, who is in third grade, is constantly being given practice tests at school to prepare her for the state assessment. It seems that in reading and math she is simply being tested, rather than actually being taught. I find this very upsetting! Why test at all? I never had to go through this when I went to school. What should I do?

Tip: First, sit with your daughter and ask her about what she is doing in school. If she feels she is simply being tested rather than learning, schedule an appointment with the teacher to talk about this. The teacher may be able to give you a bigger picture of what's happening in the classroom.

Remember, the state assessment test gauges what your child has learned up to this point in her education. If the teacher is giving practice tests based on what is being taught, it may be that she wants to make her students feel at ease by providing test simulations. Another purpose for such "mock" tests is to see whether any students have deficiencies in the subject matter or are excelling to the point of being recommended for an advanced class at a later time.

Helping children feel comfortable with testing situations at an early age will help them down the line when they are in high school, college, and the world of work.

> *Practice tests help eliminate test stress.*

Snapshot #8: Why Justify Test Answers?

My son's fifth-grade social studies teacher is giving tests in which my son needs to write several sentences justifying his answer. I don't agree with this. Why is he being tested this way? My son studies hard and learns his facts. That's what he should be tested on. What should I do?

Justifying an answer helps students grasp the how's and why's behind the facts.

Tip: This form of testing is becoming more and more popular because it encourages critical thinking. Many times there is more than one way to look at a problem, more than one answer to a question. When students are asked to state their reasons for the answer they give, they are learning much more than just how to memorize facts. They develop the ability to think for themselves and apply what they have learned to solve a problem—a valuable tool in the real world.

Snapshot #9: Why Test at All?

My daughter is in kindergarten and I really cannot understand why she is going to be given tests. I never got tested in kindergarten; in fact, all we did was play. I don't understand why the teacher needs to test at all. What should I do?

Tip: Testing helps build a learning map for your child. Tests are not given just for the sake of testing, but rather to understand what skills your child has acquired. The skills learned in kindergarten are necessary for building a solid foundation of academic success. Testing creates a record of academic performance and can also give the parent, teacher, and student a clear picture of what skills have not been learned, what skills need to be reviewed, and what skills the child has advanced in. Schedule a meeting with your daughter's teacher to review what tests will be given and the rationale for those tests.

Snapshot #10: Are Timed Tests Valid?

My son was given a timed math test and only had forty-five minutes to complete it. Is this valid? What should I do?

Tip: More and more teachers are giving students timed tests, which add another dimension to test-taking. One of the goals in giving the timed tests is to practice for the standardized practice situation. Some kids really get nervous when they have to sit and take a standardized timed test if they have never had practice of working under the pressure of time. Doing a simulation will allow your son to know what is expected. By having to complete the test within a certain time limit, your child will learn how to develop strategies to handle the challenges that come with timed tests. He will also be better prepared when he must take college entrance exams and aptitude tests later on in his academic career. Supporting your child in practicing for timed tests will help him acquire the ability to manage and successfully complete them.

Snapshot #11: What Is the Purpose of a Writing Test?

My daughter, who is in fourth grade, is taking a writing assessment at her school this year. It seems that all she does lately is write and write and write some more. I don't think that this is good teaching. How can I approach her teacher? What should I do?

Tip: Writing is an important part of your daughter's school curriculum. Writing skills are essential for succeeding in school and doing well in college and beyond. Standardized tests for college acceptance such as the SAT always contain a writing component. Be thankful that your daughter's teacher is helping her become a good writer. You may want to call the teacher to hear about what else your daughter is learning in class, and to see how you can help with your daughter's writing at home. This would be a positive way to approach the teacher and open the lines of communication.

Snapshot #12: How Can Essay Tests Be Graded?

My son will be taking an essay test this year in all of his final exams, including art, music, and physical education. What is the purpose of an essay test? How can such a test be graded objectively? I am really having a hard time with this. What should I do?

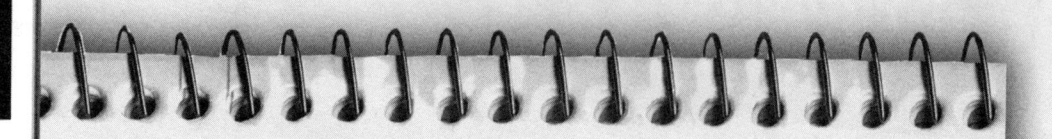

Tip: Essay tests are a good way for your son to express himself. Writing is an important part of the school program. Having the opportunity to answer questions in an essay format will assist your child later on in life. To write well, a person must think rather than simply restate memorized facts. Have your son use the following essay writing guide to prepare for his essay tests.

- What does the question ask? Did you answer the specific question asked in the essay?
- Did you answer the major points of the question and support your answer with examples and facts from the book or other valid source?
- Did you stick to the question and not go off on a tangent?
- Is your handwriting clear and legible?

Types of Tests

Type of Assessment	Purpose	Examples	Preparation
Achievement test	A type of standardized test that assesses the amount of content knowledge a student has mastered.	Iowa Test of Basic Skills, Stanford Achievement Tests, California Achievement Tests. ACT, SAT.	None, other than the basics of good nutrition and a good night's rest. This is a cumulative assessment of what the student has learned to this point.
Aptitude test	Measures a student's potential academic success.		Courses and test preparation aids exist to make a student comfortable with the format and provide test-taking strategies, but these do not teach content.
Chapter test	Evaluates a student's absorption of content matter in a specified amount of time.	Usually teacher-generated, although some book publishers provide chapter exams and test bank questions.	In-class discussion, lecture, activities, and assignments. Homework and project completion. Daily review. Frequent studying before test.
Essay test	Assesses a student's knowledge of content and critical-thinking ability by asking for interpretation, explanation, or argumentation of the topic.	Teacher, textbook publisher, or test producer–generated.	Continual practice with reading and writing and discussion and review provide a cumulative foundation for writing successful essays.
High-stakes test	Produces a consequence based on a student's achievement.	Standardized achievement tests, graduation exams, admittance exams.	None; these are cumulative exams based on a student's acquired knowledge.
Performance test	Measures a student's ability to perform a certain skill or demonstrate mastery of knowledge.	Playing a piece on a musical instrument; illustrating a mathematical concept on the board; writing an essay.	Continual study and practice.
Standardized test	Assesses a student's achievement in specific content areas with relation to a national group of peers.	Iowa Test of Basic Skills, Stanford Achievement Tests, SAT, ACT, Stanford-Binet Intelligence Scale.	None; these are cumulative exams based on a student's acquired knowledge.

Make It Happen Test on "Why Test?"

Let's see how good you are at taking tests. Review this chapter and then take the following test on the purpose of testing. You'll find the answers at the back of the book.

Directions: Read each question carefully and write your answer in the space provided after each question.

1. What does an achievement test measure?

2. List three reasons for take-home tests.

3. Why are practice tests given?

4. Explain why teachers are giving students more tests these days.

5. What are timed tests, and why are they given?

Notes:

CHAPTER TWO
Savvy Study Skills

"It's not what you know. It's what you do when you don't know!"
Albert Einstein

Taking tests often involves (or should involve) the need for extra studying at home. This chapter will provide you with no-hassle tips, techniques, and advice for improving your child's approach to studying and also provide ideas on helping your child with listening and note-taking in school. By using the charts and activities presented here, you will become familiar with what your child needs to know and do for lifelong academic success.

Start off by taking the Study Habits Quiz (see Snapshot #13) and find out whether your child has well-organized or sloppy study habits. Good study skills are important if your child is to reach his highest potential.

This chapter will address:

- Creating positive study habits
- How to study
- Where to study
- How often to study
- How to prepare for a test

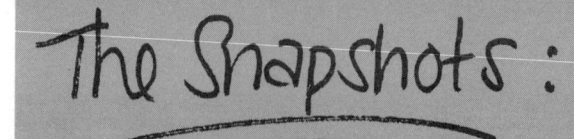

The Snapshots:

13. My Child Says He Studies, But You Wouldn't Know It by His Test Scores
14. My Child Gets Frustrated and Needs Advice on How to Study
15. My Child Takes Very Thorough Notes But Still Receives Poor Test Grades
16. My Child's Class Notebook Is a Mess and Studying for Tests Is a Challenge
17. How Can I Help My Child Study If I Am Never Home?
18. My Child Has Trouble Doing Math Word Problems on Tests
19. My Child Has Difficulty Memorizing Facts for Tests
20. My Child Spends Too Much Time Studying and I Don't See the Results on Tests
21. My Child Listens to Loud Music When Studying
22. Studying for a Test Is a Constant Battle in My House
23. My Child Needs a Tutor to Raise Test Scores
24. My Child Always Seems to Cram for Major Exams
25. Although My Child Studies with a Friend, Her Test Results Are Low
26. How Can I Help My Child Study for a Test?

Snapshot #13: My Child Says He Studies, But You Wouldn't Know It by His Test Scores

My son had a social studies test last week. When I asked him prior to the test whether he had studied, he told me he had and I took his word. When he brought home the test paper for me to sign, I was appalled at how many wrong answers he had gotten. I had to question whether he had lied to me about studying. Regardless, I was extremely disappointed in his grade and in his performance. I am now worried that his final grade will drop. What should I do?

Tip:

Step 1: First, take the following Study Habits Quiz. Find out what your child's study habits are and determine those areas that need to be changed. Ask yourself these questions: What am I doing wrong? How can I fix this? How will I approach my child? How will I set new criteria for studying and then enforce these new rules?

Step 2: Once you have analyzed the results and determined the changes that need to be made, sit down with your son and state your new expectations. Explain both your role and his. Most importantly, tell him that this is a new beginning and a new policy that will include consequences and rewards. Tell your child to remember the three B's:

- *Be* prepared to deal with study hassles.
- *Be* patient.
- *Be* consistent.

> *Change doesn't happen overnight, nor does it always go smoothly.*

Study Habits Quiz

Directions: Circle true if the statement describes your child's studying habits, circle false if it does not.

True	False	1. My child does his homework with the television on.
True	False	2. My child constantly interrupts his studying to get snacks.
True	False	3. I hear music and the phone ringing when my child says he is studying.
True	False	4. The homework planner/journal from school is a mess and test dates are not posted.
True	False	5. My child has afterschool activities every day and never misses a day.
True	False	6. I never see my child reviewing class work.
True	False	7. My child claims, "I know all the work, so why do I have to review?"
True	False	8. My child gets "test stress."
True	False	9. Studying for a test is always left to the night before.
True	False	10. Sometimes my child informs me that he has two tests in one day and hasn't prepared for either one of them.
True	False	11. My child would rather be outside playing than inside completing his assignments and studying.
True	False	12. My child studies when he feels like it.
True	False	13. My child is satisfied with quickly completing his work.
True	False	14. My child couldn't care less about his grades.

Tally your score. If it shows more "true" than "false" responses, then it is time to read the snapshots, tips, and sidebars in this book to assist you in turning things around. Implementing a schedule, designating a quiet place for homework and studying, and reinforcing the importance of concentrating on classroom instructions need to become the "new norm" for your child. Start to make changes before the backward slide gets so long and steep that it will be hard to get back on track.

Test Talk! • Understanding the Stakes and Helping Your Children Do Their Best

Snapshot #14: My Child Gets Frustrated and Needs Advice on How to Study

My child arrived home from school very upset, yelling, "Another test!" I know when I was growing up no one liked taking tests, and I guess that hasn't changed much. But back then tests were given occasionally. Children today seem to be tested constantly, and the results carry serious consequences. Many tests are mandated by the school district or state and federal governments and are tied to a student's promotion to the next grade level. Scores are compared to those of fellow classmates and to children nationwide. It is becoming more and more important that all children learn how to take tests and do well on them, and I am worried about my daughter's success. What should I do?

> *When it comes to tests, your child should follow the Boy Scout motto: Be prepared!*

Tip: To avoid getting thrown by every new test, your child needs to learn how to plan for tests well ahead of time. Different tests may need to be tackled in different ways, but it is how and when your child prepares that will make a difference on her test scores. Make a test-taking schedule with your child and make sure that she sticks to it. Planning and studying will increase your child's preparedness for all tests. You may want to refer to the Weekly Study Plan and the Weekly Study Schedule Worksheets, which follow, to help your child better prepare for tests.

Tip: Minimum preparation and study time for a test is at least one week prior to the test. Never let your child leave studying to the last minute.

Sample Weekly Study Plans

Directions: Get a blank monthly calendar for your child. Using a brightly colored marker, have him write in test dates as soon as his teacher lets him know one is coming up. Have him plan how much studying needs to be done for each subject and how much time needs to be spent on review. Then create a daily schedule with your child for the calendar, including homework and study times along with outside activities. This schedule will help your child manage the test preparation process, as well as his regular homework and other activities. Following are examples of schedules your child can create.

Sample Weekday Study Schedule

4:30 P.M.	Do homework.
7:00 P.M.	Review class notes for all subjects: Read, highlight key words, make flash cards, take notes on the important facts, go over key points with a parent.
8:00 P.M.	Study [the particular subject that will be tested]: Make practice tests, review flash cards, memorize the important facts, go over old exams, read over class notes and textbook chapters.

Sample Weekly Study Plans, Cont'd.

Sample Seven-Day Study Schedule

Monday	Tuesday	Wednesday	Thursday	Friday	Weekend
4:30 P.M. Do homework.	4:30 P.M. Do homework.	4:00 P.M. Go to soccer practice.	4:30 P.M. Do homework.	Review/study.	
7:00 P.M. Review all class work.	7:00 P.M. Review all class work.	7:00 P.M. Review all class work.	7:00 P.M. Study for test.	Review all class work for one hour each day.	
7:30 P.M. Study for social studies test.	7:30 P.M. Study for social studies test.	7:30 P.M. Study for social studies test.	7:30 P.M. Study for social studies test.		

Note: Review means you should highlight important facts/concepts, take notes on textbook content, make flash cards on the important facts that need to be memorized, and then ask Mom or Dad to quiz you on what you reviewed.

Sample Seven-Day Study Schedule Worksheet

Directions: Use this weekly study schedule to write in test dates, projects, homework, and study times, along with outside activities.

Time	Monday	Tuesday	Wednesday	Thursday	Friday	Saturday	Sunday
4:30							
5:00							
5:30							
6:00							
6:30							
7:00							
7:30							
8:00							
8:30							
9:00							

Tip: Making a list will help you prioritize what your child needs to study. Ask, "Is there a quiz tomorrow? A project due next week?" Prioritize the list and stick to it. This way you help your child make sure that everything gets done. And using a highlighter to highlight those days on the calendar when there will be a test helps visually imprint these important times. Some children stick to a schedule better if they have a checklist to use. They can put a check mark next to each accomplishment as they complete one part of a studying task. For some, breaking expectations into smaller parts produces better results.

Snapshot #15: My Child Takes Very Thorough Notes But Still Receives Poor Test Grades

My son has an organized, neatly written and dated class notebook. It appears that he has written down practically everything the teacher has said during each lesson. He knows where everything is located, because he has a heading on every page, along with subheadings. Yet his test grades are poor. What should I do?

Tip: Your child may be taking class notes daily, but is he taking these notes effectively? Writing down everything the teacher says is more likely to block out important points, making his note-taking more of a liability than a help. Knowing how to take good notes is an invaluable skill, and one that can be learned. You can help your child master this skill in a number of ways:

1. Give your child oral directions for traveling to a certain place, such as a friend's house. Then have him write down the "main concept" of the directions, rather than the details.
2. Read with him nightly, then ask him to tell you the main idea. Start simply at first with a paragraph, then go on to a page, then to a short story. You may want to take turns reading and picking out the main idea.
3. Have your child reread his notes and then rewrite them including only the important facts, along with backup information. The idea is for him to eliminate the unnecessary information. Rewriting notes is also a great tool for studying and remembering.

Tip: When learning is interactive and gamelike, children are more willing to participate. Make a few bingo cards with the weekly spelling or vocabulary words. Write the words in each square and also on small pieces of paper; place the papers in a box. Each of you takes a bingo card. Then, have your child pick one piece of paper from the box, read it out loud, and then, if it is also on his bingo card, cover that word. But he can't cover it until he turns it over and spells the word without looking at it. The entire family can play.

> *Start by breaking larger tasks into small, easy-to-accomplish steps. By following through on the small steps, your child can complete even the largest task.*

Snapshot #16: My Child's Class Notebook Is a Mess and Studying for Tests Is a Challenge

My daughter's notebook is a mess. There are drawings and scribbles on most of the pages. One page has her writing journal on it with math underneath and behind that page is a social studies quiz. When I asked her to find me her most recent math lesson on multiplication, it took her about fifteen minutes to locate it. There were no dates, so I didn't even know if that was the right page. If her notebook is such a disorganized mess, how is she supposed to study for tests or review her notes? What should I do?

Tip: Buy composition books with different color covers and then purchase folders that match those colors. Have your child pick a color for each subject. For example, label the red notebook and matching red folder "Math." Do this for all the subjects. Once this is done, instruct your child to do three things with her class work:

1. Date each page of work she completes.
2. Write each subject's notes and work in the appropriate notebook.
3. Place all take-home papers and returned tests in the proper colored folder.

This should cut down on some of the disorganization. Expect some mistakes in the beginning, but keep reinforcing the importance of doing this correctly if she wants to see better test scores. The next step is to teach your child to review her notes every night. Have different colored highlighters on hand. Let her pick two colors—for example, yellow and blue. Then, as she reviews her notes, have her highlight the key words with one color and the concepts she doesn't understand with the other. This way you can sit down with her every night and help her strengthen her study skills. The ultimate goal is that she be able to do this on her own and come to you only when she needs additional help.

Being organized is important for school success.

Snapshot #17: How Can I Help My Child Study If I Am Never Home?

I work nights and it is hard for me to help my child study for tests. The babysitter does not speak English and cannot help him. What should I do?

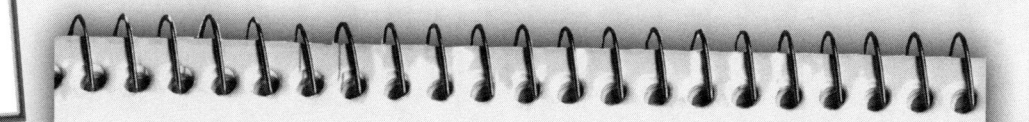

Tip: If your child is old enough, you can use a tape recorder to tape review questions and make up mock tests. Then, while you're away at work, your child can play your tape and test himself or have the babysitter turn it on and off for him. He can then check his own answers. This technique is especially helpful for children who learn best by hearing information. You can also type out mock tests for your child to practice, and then review the answers with your child when you are home.

Snapshot #18: My Child Has Trouble Doing Math Word Problems on Tests

My child is excellent at math facts. She knows addition, subtraction, multiplication, and division. She does extremely well when I test her, when she reviews flash cards, plays computer math games, and answers timed fact tests in class. When I get back her math tests, the computation part is almost always completely correct. It is the math word problems where all the errors occur. This is consistently a problem for her. What should I do?

> **Reading is fundamental to success in all school subjects.**

Tip: To do well on math word problems, you need to be able to read and understand them. Is your child's reading skill on grade level? Maybe she is rushing through the reading portion of the math problem, or perhaps she is just not sure of the key words that may help her determine what mathematical function she needs to perform to get the right answer. Sit down and talk to your child and ask her what she thinks she is doing wrong. Once you think you have the answer, meet with the teacher and develop a plan to assist your child. You may want to refer to the following Checklist for Test Preparation to assist you. If you think her lack of reading skills is causing the problem, tell her to slow down and read carefully, and get her extra help in or out of school so she can bring up those skills. If she is rushing through the test, tell her to take her time and try to stay focused. There are many tricks and tips to help with math word problems that someone—a teacher or tutor—can help your daughter learn. For example, if the problem says "in all," then addition is usually the function required; if the problem compares two items, then subtraction is usually the necessary function.

Checklist for Test Preparation

Directions: Make up a checklist like this one and share it with your child, especially when your child is experiencing difficulty with a particular skill or subject. Many of these pointers can be used for most subjects.

❏ Prepare for the test at least a week prior to taking it.

❏ Practice every night. Use the problems in the textbook or buy a commercial workbook.

❏ Listen to the teacher in class. Ask questions when you don't understand. There are probably other students having the same problem.

❏ Read carefully during the test. Don't rush!

❏ Answer the easy questions first and then go back to the hard ones.

❏ Visualize what the question wants you to do.

❏ Reread the question, and just like when you read a story, underline the key phrases and important information.

❏ Always check your answers before turning in your test.

Snapshot #19: My Child Has Difficulty Memorizing Facts for Tests

My child doesn't do well on tests. He has difficulty memorizing facts. We use flash cards, I quiz him, he rereads the books and his notes, but nothing seems to help. He is failing and his self-esteem is low. I don't know what to do for him. What should I do?

Tip: Schedule a conference with the teacher as soon as possible. Bring written questions with you so you don't forget important information that you want to discuss during the conference. Ask what she, as a teacher, would suggest to make studying easier and more meaningful for your son and how you both can help. Ask how other school personnel may be able to help as well.

Tip: As always, if you can make studying fun for your child, it becomes less of a chore and easier to master. Make a board game similar to your child's favorite game. Have study questions posted on index cards. As your child rolls the dice, he can only move ahead on the board if he answers the question correctly. The first one to the finish line is the winner. If time is pressing and you can't make a board game, you can also take index cards and put the answer on the front and the question on the back. Take turns rolling the dice and answering the test questions. If your child misses a question, give him the correct response and have him take another turn. Give two points for correct answers. The winner is the person with more points.

Study Tricks

Acronyms. Using acronyms is a good way to remember information. An acronym is a word that is formed from the first letter of each fact to be remembered. It can be a real word or a nonsense word you are able to pronounce. For example, if your child needs to memorize the five Great Lakes (Lake Huron, Lake Ontario, Lake Michigan, Lake Erie, and Lake Superior) show her how she can take the first letter of each lake and make up the word HOMES.

Word rhymes. Another study trick is to make up word rhymes. Word rhymes can make difficult concepts easier to understand. For example, division is a difficult concept when it is first introduced. Your child can remember the steps in division by creating a word rhyme with the members of a "family." The steps are Dad-divide, Mom-multiply, Sister-subtract, and Brother-bring down.

37 divided by 3. Divide (dad)—how many 3s are in 3?

Multiply (mom)—3×1

Subtract (sister)—3 take away 3

Bring down (brother)—bring down the 7 then repeat the steps

Divide (dad)—how many 3s are in 7?

Multiply (mom) $3 \times 2 = 6$

Subtract (sister) $7 - 6 = 1$

Bring down (brother)—bring down the number 1, which then becomes the remainder

Word associations. A good technique for memorization and studying is word association. When you associate, you make the things you want to remember relate to each other in some way. For example, the "principal" of a school is spelled with the word "pal" at the end. The principal is your "pal."

Visualization. Visualizing helps your child develop a strong memory. Have your child picture in her mind what she needs to remember. For example, the word "look" has two o's, which may appear as two eyes.

Snapshot #20: My Child Spends Too Much Time Studying and I Don't See the Results on Tests

My child spends quite a bit of time studying right before a test. However, his grades aren't as high as they should be, considering the amount of time that it looks like he is spending on his schoolwork. When I question him, he says he is studying. What should I do?

Encourage your child to be confident enough to ask for help in the areas he does not understand.

Topic: Studying habits
Problem: Not knowing how to study
Solution: Tips to help make a child's studying more efficient

Have your child:

- Highlight or circle those sections of his class notes he is unsure about.
- Use colored pens to write important vocabulary words or phrases in the margins of the pages of his class notes.
- Write down the numbers of the pages in the textbook that contain information he doesn't quite understand.
- Call a classmate if something seems unclear. Maybe your child wasn't focused enough in class and just needs to ask a friend for the information.
- Ask you for help if he's having a problem.
- Ask a teacher if she can review the information with him before or after class, or perhaps review a particular concept with the entire class. Your child may not be the only one who is unsure about some of the information presented.

Tip: Question him further. Ask him how he is studying, what his techniques are, and how you can assist. A good suggestion is to have him highlight important points in his notes and then question him orally on all the information, concentrating on the topics designated with the highlighter. Also ask him to put a question mark with a marker next to those sections of his notes that he is unsure about. Have him write down the pages in his textbook that contain information he doesn't understand or has questions on as well. Maybe you can assist him in the areas where he is weak, or either he or you can ask his teacher to review them with him. It is important for him to concentrate on the parts he is uncertain about as well as spend time on the areas where he is strong. You can also make up a practice test for him. Some children learn best when they are asked questions orally; others learn best when they see and read the information. Try both methods.

Snapshot #21: My Child Listens to Loud Music When Studying

My child goes up to her room the same time every night to start on her homework and study for her weekly spelling and vocabulary quiz. Unfortunately, she puts on her stereo so loud it is impossible for anyone in the house to concentrate. When I yell at her to lower the volume, she puts on her headphones. I'm worried because she is barely passing her classes, and sometimes she fails quizzes. I know I sound old-fashioned, but maybe if the music were turned off, her grades would go up as high as the volume on her stereo. What should I do?

> Where your child studies has an impact on how well she'll be able to prepare for tests.

Topic: Best ideas on how to study for a test
Problem: Knowing how to study and prepare for a test
Solution: Helpful tools students can use to prepare for a test

Have your child:

- Create a special study space that has the following: no distractions (quiet area), a large desk, a place to keep supplies (highlighters; index cards; extra paper, pens, pencils), and good ventilation.
- Make a studying calendar to highlight when exams are scheduled and help him stick to a set schedule (see Snapshot #14).
- Keep all assignments and test dates in a planner or memo pad.
- Review schoolwork daily, even if he doesn't have a test the next day.
- Ask questions during lessons.

Tip: Children study best in a quiet, comfortable place that's free from distractions. Ask yourself, "Will my child perform better on tests if she has her own studying space? Or does she need to study somewhere like the kitchen table, where I can keep an eye on her and answer any questions?" Once you decide the best spot for your child to study, let her know that you expect her to be there every night, focusing on her studies, without outside entertainment. Set an example by turning off the TV and stereos throughout the house. If you or family members must talk on the phone, keep your voices down. Make sure the study spot has good lighting, ventilation, and a comfortable chair and that there's room for your child to spread out all of her materials. Let her get started and spend some time studying on her own, because it is her responsibility to obtain higher test scores. However, be nearby in case she needs help, and always have a dictionary handy.

Snapshot #22: Studying for a Test Is a Constant Battle in My House

My teenager's test grades are F across the board. He ignores the fact that each teacher expects him to do work on his own. He has to start concentrating if he is going to do well in high school where the grades really count for his future goals. He dreams about being an Olympic swimmer and nothing else. He is already on the right tract to make this goal a reality because he has made his school's swim team and has won his first competition. I explain to him that he will still need to know how to use math, and I try to interest him by tying math to figuring out his racing time and other swimming statistics. No matter how much I yell at or nag him, I'm just not getting anywhere. I know he can do well if he applies himself. In elementary school, he was a B student. But now that he's in middle school, he seems to have an I-don't-care attitude about tests and grades. What should I do?

Tip: Before another battle begins, step back. Nagging and yelling at him and having him slam doors or ignore you aren't going to get anything accomplished. Try sitting down with him. Show him his old report cards and ask him, "How did it feel getting B's back then rather than the F's you are getting now?" Show him articles about famous sports figures who had to cut their career early because of injuries and find other jobs. Hopefully, they were smart enough to study and gain some skills to excel at other professions—whether sports-related or not. Explain to him too that one way to receive recognition and get on a college swim team is by getting a scholarship. You may want to check with his school's guidance counselor about scholarship requirements and also with the school's coach about the rules for being on a team, and especially the requirement for maintaining a certain grade point average. Explain that scholarships come from high grades and high standardized test scores together with athletic skill, and that colleges look for athletes who are also good students. Once you've stated your point of view and backed it up with facts about famous players who have had to leave sports due to injuries, allow him to state his position. However, your position must be clear: "Good grades or no sports."

> **Emphasize good grades and studying come first, then there can be time for outside activities.**

Topic: Ending studying battles
Problem: My child hates to study
Solution: Tips for avoiding studying battles

The Six B's:

1. *Be ready!* Don't react right away when your child yells back at you.
2. *Be patient!* Step back, take a deep breath, and wait for the anger to disappear.
3. *Be calm!* Keep a steady voice and maintain eye contact and start a conversation with your child.
4. *Be prepared!* Have facts ready to back up your position. Just saying "Because I said so" doesn't work.
5. *Be flexible!* Listen to hear his reasons.
6. *Be firm!* State your new rules and routines. Stick to them.

Snapshot #23: My Child Needs a Tutor to Raise Test Scores

My child is not doing well in school, either on teacher-made tests and/or book tests. The teacher seems to be trying his best to work with her, but I don't see any improvement. I tried working with her at home, but we constantly clashed and I felt our battles were ruining our relationship. On the teacher's recommendation, I decided that a tutor might be the answer. I just don't know how to go about finding the right one for my daughter. What should I do?

Tip: Ask your child's teacher if he knows about any tutoring services or private tutors. There are certain questions you need to ask when trying to locate the best tutor to suit your child's academic needs and personality. Just because your neighbor is using Miss Turnaround doesn't mean she will work well for your daughter. Interview at least two or three different tutors before you decide on one.

> *When choosing a tutor, take time and make comparisons—just as you do when buying a car.*

Guide to Working with Tutors to Solve Studying Problems

Directions: Ask your child to answer these questions. Share the answers with his teacher and tutor. It may help in understanding your child's challenges and provide clues for a solution to some of your child's studying and learning difficulties. If your child is in elementary school, do the survey with him. If your child is in middle school or high school, have him do it on his own and then share it with you or the tutor.

1. What subjects give you the most problems in school?

2. Is there one particular skill you are stuck on?

3. Do you have a plan on how to solve this problem? If so, what is it?

4. List all the ways you think you can improve.

5. Pick the best solution you can carry out and make a time line to change your studying habit, and expect to stick with it. If you can't do it alone, get assistance from your tutor.

Snapshot #24: My Child Always Seems to Cram for Major Exams

My child always crams for exams. I know that this is not the best way to get good test results and should only be used as a last resort. There is no way that anyone can read, review, and study all the necessary information in one night. He insists that this is how he likes to study, and besides, his time is limited since he belongs to so many school clubs. I know he listens in class, because his grades are passing, but he could be excelling if he just put in the effort. What should I do?

> *Time is of the essence; leaving important tasks until the last minute often results in unfavorable consequences.*

Tip: Explain to your child that you are proud of his accomplishments in his club involvement and appreciate that he is so well-rounded, but you are concerned about some of his grades. See if you can reach an arrangement. Perhaps on nights before a test, he can leave a club meeting early; or maybe he can cut out some of the clubs he is in, remaining only in the ones that interest him most. Explain that you would like him to succeed in both his outside interests and his test results. Let him know that cramming is a short-term fix and that although he may pass this test, he will most likely not retain the information in the long run.

Cramming may become an option when:

1. More than one test is being given on the same day.
2. Your child forgot about a test even though the teacher announced the date several times.
3. Your child wrote the wrong test day down in the planner.
4. The teacher announced a possible surprise quiz.

Guide to Cramming for Exams

Directions: Check off each cramming technique as you complete it. Remember that cramming for an exam only affords you the opportunity to study the important facts. Your goal is to pass the test, not retain all the information that was covered.

- ❏ Get a highlighter or marker and get ready to review class notes. Highlight the important facts and main points that the teacher emphasized in class.

- ❏ Call a friend and ask him what he thought were the most important facts he thinks will appear on the test.

- ❏ Keep the highlighter handy and review the textbook. Rewrite and highlight in your class notes the definitions, equations, and names that are shown in bold print in the textbook. Such points are usually on an exam, and copying them down is a good study tool.

- ❏ Be a clock keeper. Figure out how much time you really have to study for the test. After highlighting, review and repeat the material you deem most important. Repeat again and again only the important facts.

- ❏ Outline the key points. Put them in priority order of what you know and what you need to study again. This will help you budget your time.

- ❏ Divide a blank sheet of paper in half. Make up your own questions on one side of the paper, and on the other side answer the questions. Use this technique as a studying tool. Some of the questions can come from the end of the textbook chapter.

Snapshot #25: Although My Child Studies with a Friend, Her Test Results Are Low

My child studies continually with a friend at either our home or her friend's or over the phone. I do overhear them mention the test and ask each other some questions, but the bulk of the time is spent on gossip and social issues of the day. If the test was on who's who at school or what's happening in the cafeteria, she would get an A. How do I get her to stick to the real subject matter? What should I do?

Tip: Discuss with your daughter the importance of studying to earn high test scores. Tell her you do not mind her studying with a buddy, but there are certain strategies they can use to do well on a test. Suggest these simple tricks:

- Have them quiz each other on practice questions at the end of each chapter.
- Have each child make up an exam and then give it to the study partner.
- Ask each child to make up study or flash cards and exchange them.
- Suggest they compare class notes to see if they agree on the important content the teacher stressed in class; have them highlight important facts on which they both agree.
- Recommend that they review the textbook chapters and ask each other to explain the words or concepts that are highlighted.

> *If test scores remain low, maybe it is time to take privileges away until the results improve.*

Snapshot #26: How Can I Help My Child Study for a Test?

As a parent I just don't know how best I can assist my child in studying. We always review the night before by answering questions orally, but I am wondering if there is any other way I can help my child? What should I do?

Tip: Speak with the teacher to see if she has any suggestions. One technique is to create a sample test as a studying tool. There are a few different ways to do this. You can make up a test on your own, which usually works well with younger children. For older children, the student can make his own test if he is receptive to the idea—a great way to reinforce what was learned! Encourage him to correct the test himself, then go back and review the material for those questions he answered incorrectly. A third way is to use a practice test, usually found at the end of the chapter in a textbook. Any of these methods are effective in helping your child learn and maintain important material.

Make It Happen Test on "Savvy Study Skills"

Let's see how good you are at taking tests. Review this chapter and take the following test on developing your child's study skills in order to help him or her prepare for tests. You'll find the answers at the end of the book.

Directions: Fill in the blank spaces to complete each statement.

1. A student should study at least _____ in advance in order to be best prepared for a test.

2. Techniques you can use to assist your child in memorizing facts are:

   _____

   _____

3. To avoid a last-minute studying crunch, the child and parent should make and display a

   _____.

4. During a test, advise your child to answer the _____ first and save the

   _____ for last.

5. A highlighter can assist as a studying tool to specify _____ and _____.

Notes:

CHAPTER THREE
No Test Stress!

"Tension is who you think you should be. Relaxation is who you are."
Chinese proverb

Now that you understand the reasons behind testing and have created a solid studying foundation for your child, how can you eliminate test stress? Be prepared! Show your child your support and commitment, then follow through to help reduce test anxiety and increase positive results.

This chapter will provide tips, strategies, and techniques for worried parents and stressed-out children. Some of the important information we'll address:

- The school's role in testing
- A countdown to test success

The Snapshots:

27. My Child Is Only in First Grade, Yet He Is Showing Signs of Test Stress
28. Special Foods for Special Needs
29. My Son Threw Up on His Test
30. Too Many Tests on the Same Day
31. I Tend to Stress Out Myself and My Child About Tests
32. My Child Fails Tests and It's Affecting Her Grades
33. My Child Is Stressing Me Out
34. The Amount of Testing—and Stress—Seems to Increase with Each Grade
35. Multiple Choice Tests Confuse My Child
36. It's a Battle to Get My Daughter to Study for a Test
37. The School Has Sped Up the Curriculum to Cover the Test

Test Talk! • Understanding the Stakes and Helping Your Children Do Their Best

Snapshot #27: My Child Is Only in First Grade, Yet He Is Showing Signs of Test Stress

My child completed kindergarten successfully and is now in the second half of first grade. He came home with a paper stating he will be taking a standardized test in two months. His teacher is going to give practice tests and drills daily. Her feeling is that my child will be put at ease when the real thing is placed in front of him. But my first-grader has reacted in the opposite way. He's become anxious about the test, thanks in part to his older brother, who keeps saying the test is really hard and my younger son will probably have to do first grade all over again. My son is a wreck and so am I. Why are they testing so much? What should I do?

> *The more experience a child has in taking different types of tests, the more confidence he will have to meet the challenge of any testing situation.*

Tip: The teacher is correct in this case. Testing of our children is not going to go away. It allows for school accountability and gives us knowledge of just how well each child is succeeding.

Yes, there are other means of measuring progress, but we need to see the total child, and test scores give us an important part of the picture. Under NCLB, students are given standardized tests in grades 3–8 and once in high school. Many states are also giving first- and second-graders standardized tests to determine children's progress and if they are making learning gains or need extra help before third grade.

One good way to reduce test stress is to have students practice, practice, and practice some more. This will give your child the skills he needs to be able to deal with all kinds of testing formats and the confidence to get through any test situation. Practice will help him understand how to fill in a bubble answer, how to read directions carefully, how to eliminate the obvious wrong answers in a multiple choice question, and how to organize his thoughts for a written response. Here are a few other steps you can take to help prevent test stress:

- Leave a note in your child's backpack, notebook, or lunch box reminding him that you love him and just want him to do his best.
- Encourage your child to dance, jump, or wiggle around the kitchen before leaving for school. Any kind of physical activity is a warm-up for the body and the mind and might ease any stress beginning to build up. (Of course, it's a great laugh for the kids when their parents dance, jump, or wiggle with them!)
- Allow your child to buy a special package of No. 2 pencils to be used during testing. Just knowing that these are his own special items might make him feel more confident.

Topic: Testing young children
Problem: The dreaded first test
Solution: Student guidelines for test-taking

> *A first response is usually the correct one.*

Have your child:

1. Make a calendar of test dates. Update it as soon as the teacher announces the date and type of test she'll be giving. This way your child can see at a glance when a test is approaching and then budget review and studying times.
2. Prepare his backpack the night before the test, with all the materials he will need for the test.
3. Get a good night's sleep. Have him go to bed earlier than usual so he can get up earlier and review notes once in the morning.
4. Eat a healthy breakfast on the day of the test. Have him go light on the high-sugar foods.
5. Find out how much time is allotted for the test and plan about how much time he will have for each section.
6. Find out how much each section is worth.
7. Skim the entire test first.
8. Read the directions carefully. If the test asks him to read a section and then answer questions, remind him to read the questions first. Then, while he is reading the passage, he can underline the key words and ideas the questions refer to.
9. Look for key words, such as "more," "less," "in all," and "evenly," if the test has math word problems.
10. Answer the questions he finds to be the easiest first. Remind him not to linger too long on a problem that is giving him difficulty. Suggest he put a circle around its number and come back to it. If he doesn't have time to answer it during the test, when the time is almost up, he can go back and take an "educated guess."
11. Once he is finished have him review the entire test for silly mistakes. Remind him not to change an answer unless he is absolutely sure he made an error.

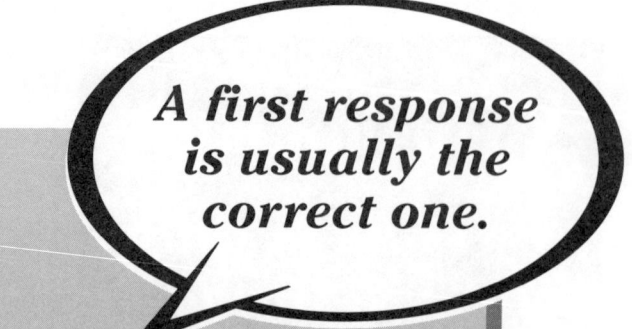

Snapshot #28: Special Foods for Special Needs

My daughter is in fourth grade and has a hard time focusing. Because of this she does not do well on tests. She will be taking the state assessment this year and I have heard that having her eat certain foods will help her keep focused and reduce stress. What types of food should I feed her? What should I do?

Tip: Make sure your child is eating healthy foods at every meal. Try to keep high-sugar foods and foods with artificial coloring out of her diet. Also, see if she can bring a healthy snack with her the day of the test in case she gets a break between testing sections.

Tip: Make sure that the school is providing all the necessary accommodations for students according to the IDEA (Individuals with Disabilities Education Improvement Act) and their individual IEPs (Individualized Education Plan). Children with special needs are allowed special adaptations for test situations and class instruction. These are written down and given to the parent so you know what accommodations are provided for your child on the days of standardized testing and routine teacher tests. These accommodations are put in place specifically for your child's school success.

Snapshot #29: My Son Threw Up on His Test

Every time my son hears the word "test" he becomes extremely nervous. Yesterday, he threw up on the state assessment test and his test was invalidated. It seems that he cannot take a test without freaking out. What should I do?

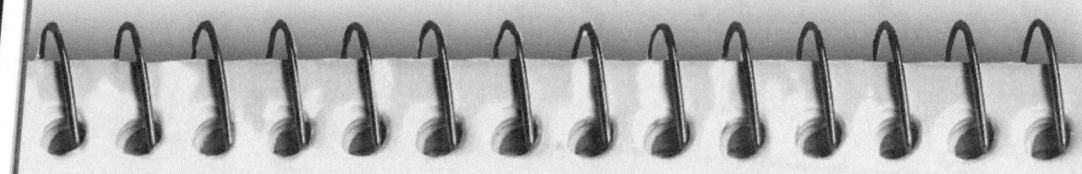

Tip: You need to help your son take a proactive approach to testing, which will reduce anxiety and build his confidence. First, sit with your child and discuss why he feels such fear. Second, talk to your child's teacher and craft a plan. Studies have shown that rehearsing a stressful event can lessen or even eliminate the fear of that event. Have the teacher send home packets to practice the testing situations he will encounter. Third, consider talking to the school counselor for other strategies you can implement to help him. Unfortunately, standardized tests can not be retaken. However, there might be an alternative test your child can take at a later date. Try also the following tips to get your son on the road to stressless testing:

- *On an ongoing basis:* Create an affirmation with your child to ease his stress. A good affirmation is "I am ready for this test and I will do just fine." Have him say it several times a day or when he feels the stress coming upon him.
- *Several days before the test:* Devise a plan of action. Have your child review the material that he has already learned.
- *The night before the test:* Instead of having your child study, ask him to do a quick review. At this point he knows what he knows. Reviewing will reinforce confidence in your child. After that is completed, have him get to bed as early as possible to get a good night's sleep.
- *The day of the test:* Get your child up early. Provide a good breakfast and leave the house with time to spare. Being hungry or rushed only adds to stress.
- *During the test:* Have your child take a deep breath and repeat his affirmation before he starts.
- *After the test:* Congratulate your child for doing his best and plan to do something fun and relaxing as a reward.

Snapshot #30: Too Many Tests on the Same Day

My child came home today all stressed out because she has three big chapter tests in math, social studies, and science on the same day. She is totally overwhelmed, and I don't blame her. It's not fair to students to pile up the tests on one day like this. What should I do?

Tip: Many schools have testing calendars to prevent just this type of problem. However, since your school does not, this is an opportunity for your daughter to learn a life lesson: Sometimes life isn't fair and she has to come up with a strategy to do her best when faced with a difficult situation.

Sit with your child and go over the tests that will be given. Make sure that in the future your child marks all tests on a calendar and studies a little each night. Divide up her time with the subject that needs the most attention. You may assist her by gathering all the materials she needs for studying and dividing them into the three subjects on which she'll be tested. Place the books, pencils, textbooks, notes, and review sheets into piles. Now it is up to her to highlight and review the most important facts from each subject area and make study sheets for review the next day. When she is finished with each subject, be available to ask her questions on the material orally.

Make plans to get up earlier in the morning so you can give her a quick quiz from her study sheets. Tell her to keep these sheets handy so that prior to each test, she can look them over and have the most important facts fresh in her mind.

When the day of the tests is finally over and she is ready to let you know how it went, you can have a talk with her about time management and a study schedule. However, use your judgment on her mood and receptivity; you may want to put off this talk for a few days if she needs to wind down before getting a lecture from you.

> *Pick the appropriate times to discuss important matters such as time management and better studying strategies for earning good test scores.*

Snapshot #31: I Tend to Stress Out Myself and My Child About Tests

My child has special needs but is doing well in school. I tend to push him hard and I know this is why he is doing well. I met with his teacher and she told me this year he will have to take a state assessment. I don't know if he can succeed on this type of test, and I am really stressed about this. What should I do?

Stay calm around your child when he is anxious about a test.

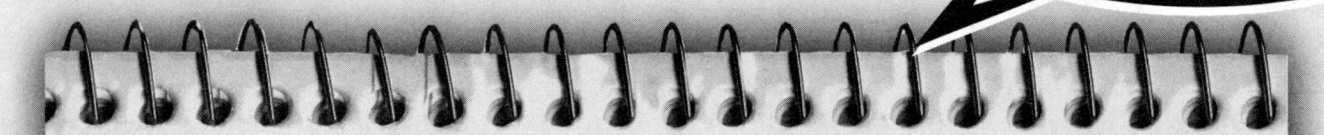

Tip: You should be commended for how well your child is doing as well as the fact that you recognize that how you act around your child will affect him and his performance. Sometimes talking with your child about a test releases some of the stress. Do not make a big deal about this state assessment. Calm yourself down by realizing that since your child is doing well in school, he will probably do well on the test. Concentrate on just making sure that your child is at his best for the test. Try some of the tips for stressless testing shown in Snapshot #29.

Snapshot #32: My Child Fails Tests and It's Affecting Her Grades

My child does well on her class work, but refuses to study for tests. Her attitude is that tests don't make a difference. I know they do and try to make her understand this. Because of her poor test scores, she just brought home a terrible report card, which is unacceptable. I make sure she does her homework and I quiz her every night on some of her class work, yet she refuses to study for tests. What should I do?

Tip: First, don't lose your cool. Calmly let your daughter know that you are disappointed. Applaud any grades that were good and tell her that studying for tests is nonnegotiable. Second, try to find out the reason she dislikes studying for tests so much. Call for a teacher conference with both your child and you. See what the teacher feels is causing this attitude of hers. Once the reasons are narrowed down, then come up with strategies.

> *Always be prepared for a conference. Bring along report cards and other school documentation (see the documentation templates in Chapter Five) you have collected as a starting point for a good conference discussion.*

Snapshot #33: My Child Is Stressing Me Out

When it comes to taking tests, my child always knows the material covered, but he is extremely lacking in self-confidence. He frets that he won't do well, and then his fears become real. I know if he only had more self-assurance, he would do so much better on tests. What should I do?

Tip: Panic during a test can often set in when a child either feels he doesn't know the material or lacks confidence in himself as a test-taker. As a parent, you have to be honest with your son about his skills, but affirmative in your praise. You can make statements such as "I know you can ace this test. You have studied so hard and when I tested you, you knew the answers." If he's made any improvement, you could point that out: "Your studying paid off last time. Look how much your scores went up." Also let him know that you believe in his ability to improve and that you are proud of his willingness to ask for assistance when needed. It goes back to praising the effort and encouraging any small steps to increase skills as a means to build confidence, just as you did when he was a toddler, when he went from taking his first step to walking successfully on his own.

Snapshot #34: The Amount of Testing—and Stress—Seems to Increase with Each Grade

It's the end of the school year. Summer's here and our family was looking forward to taking a break from schoolwork and having some family fun. But not this summer! My daughter, who is in second grade, just informed me that she will be taking an important test next year—the state assessment test—and if she doesn't pass, she can't move up to fourth grade. Her teacher told her she'd better continue to study over the summer. We are all stressed out. I want to know the purpose of all the future tests my daughter has to take, especially the one she has to take next year. I understand that the results of these standardized tests determine whether my daughter goes on to the next grade or, when she is older, whether she graduates. What should I do?

> *Testing provides a snapshot of a child's abilities and demonstrates a student's achievement on content and specific skills.*

Tip: Go to your state's Department of Education's Web site for information on testing promotion and retention and graduation requirements. (See Appendix B.) On the Web site you should also find a calendar giving you the dates of the test administration. Being prepared for what lies ahead is important. However, remember that your child also needs a school break and summer fun is needed! Plan a day or two a week where you do some academic work with your child or even enroll her in a tutoring club.

State assessment tests give teachers, students, and parents feedback on what knowledge and skills have been mastered and what areas need more work. The goal is to have all students reach a level of proficiency, or higher, in essential subjects as measured by the state-set standards. Pretests can provide guidance on what to study and how much time needs to be devoted to skills not yet mastered. Post-tests and retests mark progress, highlighting what has been learned and what needs further studying and explanations. End-of-chapter tests that test results on specific topics inform parents, students, and teachers alike what information has been understood and retained. Many times, test outcomes give clearer insight into whether a child should continue on to the next level.

Tips for Better Test-Taking

Multiple choice tests:

Have your child:

- Read each question carefully.
- Eliminate the answers he knows are incorrect.
- If he still doesn't know which answer is correct, take a guess on the remaining choices.
- Know that his first thought or guess is usually a good one. Suggest that he not make any changes unless he is absolutely sure of the answer.
- Know that "None of the above" means that not one answer fits the question asked. Example:

    Congress meets in the
    a. White House
    b. Washington Monument
    c. Supreme Court Building
    d. None of the above

- Understand that "Some of the above" means that more than one answer fits the question asked. Often one of the choices given will combine more than one right answer. Example:

    The Declaration of Independence was written by
    a. Thomas Jefferson
    b. Benjamin Franklin
    c. Abraham Lincoln
    d. Both a. and b.
    e. Both b. and c.

- Know that "All of the above" means that all of the answers fit the question asked. Example:

    Symbols of national pride are the
    a. American flag
    b. Pledge of Allegiance
    c. Bald eagle
    d. All of the above

Short-answer tests:

Have your child:

- Memorize the key facts the teacher emphasizes in class.
- Know key words and definitions.
- Know time lines, dates, names, and formulas.
- Learn all the parts of graphs or diagrams as reviewed in class, especially in science and geography lessons. He can expect to be given a blank diagram or map and asked to label the various sections.
- Memorize dates and the correlating important events, especially in history lessons. He can be sure the teacher will include these on the test with spots for him to fill in.
- Write neatly and legibly.
- Understand that if there is more than one part to an answer, he shouldn't leave any of the parts blank. If he's not sure of an answer, he should take a guess. He may receive partial credit for any correct parts of an answer.
- Skip a question he's stuck on and come back to it after he's gone through the entire test. The answer may come to him then, or he may even find information in other

Tips for Better Test-Taking, Cont'd.

questions or answers that will help him resolve the difficult question. If the answer isn't clear, urge him to make an educated guess. Never leave an empty space.

Open-book tests:

Have your child:

- Identify the important points in the book.
- Highlight phrases in a book if allowed. If this is not allowed, have him ask the teacher if he can post sticky notes in the book.
- Make notes on a separate sheet of paper. However, be sure he asks the teacher prior to the test whether he can use these notes during the test.
- Know the facts as if the book was closed. Open-book tests are usually more difficult than regular tests.
- Answer those questions he feels confident about first, then go back to the questions for which he needs to search the book.
- When in doubt, move on, and then come back if he has time. Don't spend too much time on one question.

Essay tests:

Have your child:

- Read the directions first. Make sure he understands how many questions need to be answered. Put check marks on the questions about which he knows plenty of information and facts. Be positive and answer the essays he knows he can ace.
- Outline all the information he knows will be needed to answer the question using the margin or on scratch paper. He can number the outline points in the order he wants them to appear in the actual essay, then write the sentences and paragraphs.
- Spend time writing the information and facts, not the "fluff." Remind him that this is not a creative writing test; the teacher wants to find out how much he knows about the topic. If he is not sure about a statement, advise him to leave it out.
- Leave time to reread his answers, making sure he has gone straight to the point and has written everything pertinent that he knows. Remind him not to forget to check for spelling and grammar mistakes.
- Use a single line to cross out anything that he may have written in error. Remind him to be neat and not erase.
- Watch the clock. He needs to budget his time based on how many essays he must complete in the allotted amount of time. Remind him to do the math before he starts. For example, if he has two questions to answer in fifty minutes, have him allot about twenty minutes for each essay and ten minutes to reread and make any corrections or additions that might be needed.

Tip: Teach your child to always answer the questions he is sure of first, then go back and answer the more difficult ones. If he knows he won't be penalized, he should take a guess on questions he is not sure of and never leave a blank.

Snapshot #35: Multiple Choice Tests Confuse My Child

My child gets completely confused when he takes a multiple choice test. I have tried to help him by telling him to read each choice and take out those that don't fit. It doesn't work. Instead, he becomes stressed and frustrated. What should I do?

Tip: There is an art to testing. Although multiple choice tests are considered easier than other tests because the right answer is given as a choice, they can also be confusing if your child has not studied and understood the material. First, make sure that your child knows the material that will be tested. Second, talk to the teacher and see if he can give you some sample multiple choice tests for your son to take. These mock tests should be similar in format to the one he will be taking.

Test Talk! • Understanding the Stakes and Helping Your Children Do Their Best

Snapshot #36:
It's a Battle to Get My Daughter to Study for a Test

My daughter tends to get nervous every time I try to sit down with her and review before a test. She is a good student and gets good grades on her report card, but studying becomes a battle whenever a test comes around. How can I help her study for a test without making it such a stressful event? What should I do?

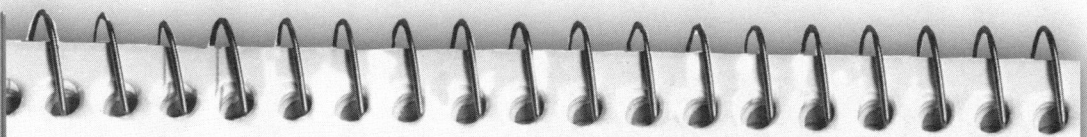

Tip: The best way for you to help your child is to have a plan and follow it. A little bit of studying on a daily basis goes a long way when a test is near. Preparing your child for tests without her even knowing it is easy. Just follow these steps:

Step 1. Do it daily! The best way to help your child truly learn something is to review her work daily. Go over her homework. Ask her questions.

Step 2. Talk about it! The more your child talks about what she heard in class, the more likely she is to remember it. Have discussions at the dinner table. Ask each person to tell something he or she learned that day. You'll be surprised how much you'll find out about your child's lessons. You'll probably also be pleasantly surprised at how much you can contribute—through your own stories, experiences, and knowledge—to what your child has already learned.

Step 3. Make note cards. Get your child to make one or two note cards a day on important concepts she has learned. (It may help to buy her a special index card file and let her paint or decorate it her own way.) Give her card dividers as well for different subjects. Then, each day, have her fill out a card or two in each subject. The mere act of writing it down helps her learn the material, and then she'll have a handy study guide for review before the test. (And it doesn't take long to write one sentence!)

Step 4. Use visual supports. Make learning progress obvious by using visual ways of supporting, monitoring, and encouraging her. Let your child put sticky notes on the refrigerator under her name to show what she's working on at school. Some families enjoy making charts that allow each child to write notes about what he or she learned. Another possibility is to make categories for history, math, English, and science, and then have your child write on a sticky note what she's studying in those subjects. (You'd be surprised at the motivational power of neon-colored sticky notes and pens!)

Step 5. Supplement. Once you know what your child is studying in school, you can supplement what she learns in the classroom by providing quality videos about that topic, taking her to the public library for additional books, and telling her about your own experiences or people she knows who might connect to those topics.

Step 6. Apply lessons learned at home. As often as possible, apply the lessons of the classroom to the "real" world so your child sees how what she's learning is relevant.

Snapshot #37: The School Has Sped Up the Curriculum to Cover the Test

My son, who is in third grade, came home with a notice that the school is getting ready to increase the amount of reading instruction to make sure that all of the skills tested on the state assessment are covered. I didn't realize that the standardized test came so early. My child is in a panic. What should I do?

Tip: Know what tests your child will be taking, what they measure, and how his scores will be used in making any decisions about your child's education. For example, will test results be used to place students in an advanced curriculum, be tutored after school, be pulled out of the classroom for extra lessons in their weak areas, or be promoted or retained? A good time to find out the answers to these questions is during Open House so you are prepared for the year ahead.

Make It Happen Test on "No Test Stress!"

Let's see how good you are at taking tests. Review this chapter and take the following test on helping prevent your child from stressing out over tests. You'll find the answers at the end of the book.

Directions: Read each question carefully and fill in the blanks.

1. List at least four test-taking strategies your child should know.
   a.
   b.
   c.
   d.
2. The best place to find a standardized testing schedule is _____.
3. When a teacher returns a test paper, your child should do four things: _____
   _____.
4. List at least three strategies for taking an essay test.
   a.
   b.
   c.
5. "It is important to know ahead of time what a test measures and how the results will affect your child's education." In a short essay, explain why this statement is important.

Notes:

CHAPTER FOUR
After the Test

"Nothing ever comes to one that is worth having except as a result of hard work."
Booker T. Washington

Your child comes home and hands you the test paper. You look at the grade given and the comments made. Now what?

That test and those comments give you a wealth of information about your child's skills and abilities, but they may also leave you asking yourself some difficult questions.

- How can you use the information given?
- Is your child making the grade?
- What can you do if your child's classroom performance doesn't match the test score?
- Is your child making learning gains?
- Can learning errors be remedied? How?

This chapter will show you how to understand test results, and it provides simple steps to help your child improve academic achievement. Establishing ongoing communication with the school will keep you informed about when and what type of tests are given. The following tips and strategies will help you ask school personnel the right questions regarding your child's assessments and academic achievement.

The Snapshots:

38. My Son Doesn't Look at His Returned Test Papers
39. My Child's Standardized Test Scores Are Dropping Each Year
40. Parent-Teacher Conferences Have Never Solved My Concerns About My Son's Previous Failed Tests and Inability to Achieve Good Scores
41. My Child Rushes Through Essay Tests
42. My Child's Tests Seem Too Easy
43. My Child Failed a Literacy Test and Will Possibly Be Retained
44. My Child Failed Another Test
45. When a Test Is Over, Is It Really Over?
46. My Child Doesn't Do Well on Quizzes
47. Help! My Child's Test Scores Are Back and I Don't Understand What They Mean
48. My Child Keeps Making the Same Types of Errors on His Tests
49. I Save Every Test That Comes Home and I Am Running Out of Room
50. My Child Earns Good Grades in School But Scores Poorly on Standardized Tests

www.school-talk.com

Test Talk! • Understanding the Stakes and Helping Your Children Do Their Best

Snapshot #38: My Son Doesn't Look at His Returned Test Papers

My child's teacher takes a lot of time marking test papers. She circles what is incorrect and sometimes puts a comment or the right answer on the paper. She truly wants the children to see what errors they made. My son doesn't pay attention to anything except the grade that appears at the top of the page. Even when he gets an A, I want him to look at his errors. What should I do?

> *One of the great benefits of making a mistake is learning from what went wrong.*

Tip: Each test that we take throughout our lives gets us ready for the next one. Have your child review his errors and correct them. If he still doesn't understand why an answer was marked wrong, have him ask his teacher. Going back to the textbook or his class notes will show him how to correct his mistakes, as well as increase his skills for the next test and for learning the next academic concept. Review the test with your child and help him find the answer to any question he is still struggling with. If the problem persists, call for a teacher conference. Make it clear that your goal is for your child to understand this concept and you need her help. Keeping a Test Results Log will help your child see how he is doing and assist you during parent-teacher conferences. See the sample in Chapter Five.

Snapshot #39: My Child's Standardized Test Scores Are Dropping Each Year

I am terribly concerned. Each year there is more and more pressure put on the teacher and the students to perform well on the state's mandatory exams. I feel like all the teacher does is teach to the test and this does not work for my child. Although she has typically been a good student overall, my child has never been a good test-taker. Now she gets test stress, and I think the teacher does too. What worries me more is that her grades on the math and reading portions have actually dropped. Even though she does well in class, her scores do not reflect what she knows. What should I do?

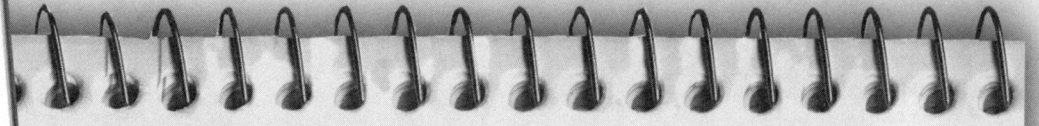

Tip: At the very start of the school year, request a conference with the teacher. Tell him you would like to discuss a strategy to help your child stay on track so she can achieve higher percentages on the standardized tests. Ask about what he has planned for the school year in test preparation skills as well as the academics. Many schools and school districts print up practice test booklets that parents can use to help their children become better test-takers. These booklets explain how to read test results and often have sample test questions for each subject and grade level. Call your school district office and ask whether they have test booklets or other resources to help you. Many states also show the state standards on their Web sites; these standards determine what questions will be on the state tests. Once you know what these standards are, you will understand which skills your child is expected to master. You can also go to your state's Department of Education Web site (see Appendix B) and download practice tests. Then keep track of your child's standardized test scores with a chart like the one shown in Chapter Five.

It's a good idea to follow up with the teacher as often as once a month, even if it is just a phone call. Don't wait to communicate with him right before the test or immediately after the new results are posted. That may be too late.

Stay on top of your child's progress all year long.

Test Talk! • Understanding the Stakes and Helping Your Children Do Their Best

Snapshot #40: Parent-Teacher Conferences Have Never Solved My Concerns About My Son's Previous Failed Tests and Inability to Achieve Good Scores

I have had many conferences with teachers about my child's test scores throughout the years my child has been in school. Unfortunately, I leave each one dissatisfied with the process and the outcome. It seems like my concerns are either not taken seriously or put off to be dealt with later, which is often too late to help my child. His learning problems are very real and he needs a specific plan, yet the school continues to take a "head-in-the-sand" approach on how to treat his needs. He squeaks by every year, acquiring the minimum skills—just enough to be promoted to the next grade. He is barely reading on grade level and his math skills are weak. Evidently the school views this as good enough, but I feel he becomes weaker in his skills each year. This year he is in third grade, and passing the state standardized test determines promotion to the next grade level. I am worried that my son will not score well enough to go to the fourth grade. How do I get help? How do I communicate with the school personnel that something has to change if my child is to become successful? I need answers and I want action. What should I do?

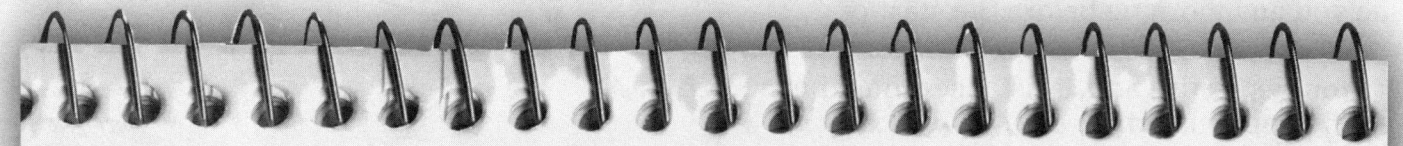

Tip: Meet with the teacher immediately and be firm in voicing your concerns. Tell her you would like to meet with the entire school team—teacher, counselor, assistant principal, and anyone else who can assist you in addressing your child's learning problems and helping him score well on tests. You may want to use the Sample Letter for Requesting a Conference (see following). Explain that you have asked for help from teachers in the past, but because the situation has not improved, you feel it is imperative to bring in others to evaluate your child's learning and test-taking skills, especially since the upcoming state test is so important to his academic future. Let her know when you are available and ask that she set up the meeting. Then use the Checklist for a Successful Conference (see page 71) to gather your thoughts, important documents, and samples of your child's work. If you don't hear from your son's teacher in two or three days, call to politely remind her. If she still fails to set up the meeting, call the school office and ask to meet with the guidance counselor, assistant principal, or the principal.

Be sure to keep a Communications Report Log (see Chapter Five) for your records.

Sample Letter for Requesting a Conference

September 21, 2007

Dear Ms. Smart,

I would like to request a conference with you regarding my son John's test-taking abilities. I'm concerned about his poor performance when testing and would like to discuss any ideas or strategies we might use that would help him in this area.

Would you please call me on my cell at (366) 286-5555 at your earliest convenience to arrange a time we could get together? I can see you any morning before the start of school.

Your expertise and assistance would be greatly appreciated.

Sincerely,

Mrs. Jones

> *It is always useful to let the teacher know before a meeting what your concerns are so he too can prepare any needed information and documentation for the conference.*

Checklist for a Successful Conference

Use this checklist to make sure you have everything you need to make the parent-teacher conference a success. Forms can be found in Chapter Five.

- ❏ Communications Report Log
- ❏ Standardized Test Tracking Sheet
- ❏ Academic portfolio: samples of class work and homework
- ❏ Report cards and progress reports
- ❏ Returned reports and tests
- ❏ Previous conference reports
- ❏ Conference Planning Form
- ❏ Test Results Log
- ❏ Prepared questions you may have
- ❏ Vision and Goals for School Success Sheet: statements of where you want your child to be at the end of the school year and in the future

Snapshot #41: My Child Rushes Through Essay Tests

My daughter, who is in fourth grade, is always in a rush to be the first one done on any test her teacher gives. When I review her returned tests, I can see how this is affecting her performance, especially on the essay questions. I am terribly worried with the state writing exam coming up that she will not be able to go on to the next grade level. If she does not get a certain passing score on this test she will be held back. I know this is a bad habit that must be changed soon so her grades improve and her true talents can shine. What should I do?

> Checklists are a great tool for your child to use to organize her writing.

Tip: Make an appointment to meet with the teacher and have your child present at the meeting. Ask the teacher to recommend strategies for your child to stay focused and complete the test successfully. Have the teacher share techniques that she has used with other students or practice books you can borrow or purchase. It takes practice to learn how to answer test questions in essay form. Give your child the following checklist to use when writing paragraphs, essays, or short answers. Once she gets used to following these steps, they will become automatic and you and your daughter will notice a difference in her writing style and her test scores. Encourage your daughter to take her time instead of rushing through tests. Sometimes just getting organized and having a set format makes all the difference.

Writing Checklist

Have your child:

Before writing:

- ❏ Read directions carefully.
- ❏ Make an outline of his thoughts on a piece of scrap paper.
- ❏ Write down all the important facts he memorized next to the outline.
- ❏ Read again and ask himself, "What exact information do I need to answer the question?"
- ❏ Outline the main sentence for each answer. Remind him to write down all the main thoughts that can lead into the paragraphs.

During writing:

- ❏ Write out the paragraph or paragraphs with all the information he listed in the outline.
- ❏ Reread the question to make sure he answered it.
- ❏ Make sure he has a beginning, a middle, and an end.
- ❏ Try to rewrite the question into his first sentence as the main idea.
- ❏ Restate the main idea as the last sentence.

Before handing in the test paper:

- ❏ Edit for grammar, capitalization, spelling, and ending punctuation.
- ❏ Check to see that each paragraph has at least five sentences and that all his statements support his main idea.
- ❏ Make sure his paragraphs are connected with words such as "first," "second," "next," "then," and "finally."

Snapshot #42: My Child's Tests Seem Too Easy

My child does well on all his tests and even the surprise quizzes his fourth-grade teacher loves to spring on his class. He told me he finished the standardized test in record time and he scored the highest possible scores on the reading, math, and writing exams. The present schoolwork is too easy for him and I constantly hear, "School is boring." What should I do?

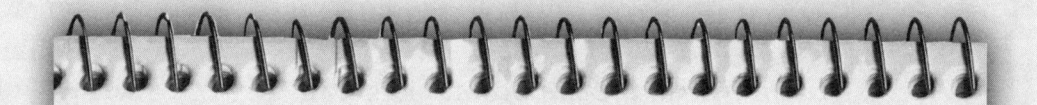

Tip: Have a conference with the teacher and ask him if there is a way he can challenge your son with extra projects or give him higher-level assignments when his regular class work is completed. Better yet, ask him if there are advanced classes or possibly a gifted program at the school so that your son is challenged when he enters fifth grade.

> *Make sure your child is always challenged in school so that he can reach his highest learning potential.*

Snapshot #43: My Child Failed a Literacy Test and Will Possibly Be Retained

My daughter has been struggling in first grade since September. I have been sending her to a tutor and she has been getting C's on her report card. Her teacher called me today to tell me that she failed the early literacy test that she was given and if she fails it again in May she will be retained. I have never heard of this test. It's only January. How can they make such a strong decision? I am not in agreement with this. What should I do?

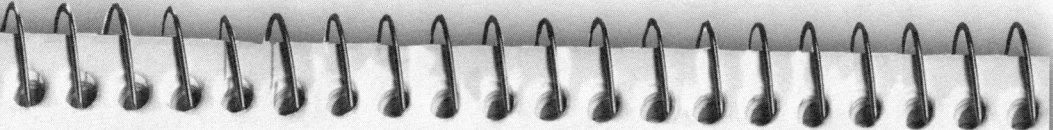

Tip: Many schools give students in the early grades a literacy test to determine their reading ability. These tests are often given orally and in a one-to-one setting, meaning the classroom teacher takes the child to a quiet area and gives the test; many of these tests are also timed. According to research conducted by the Reading Research Program at the National Institute of Child Health and Human Development (NICHD), "Simple tests of children's skill at working with phonemes could predict later reading problems and failure."

Being able to read requires phonemes and phonemic awareness. *Phonemes* are spoken words that are made up of individual pieces of sounds that are put together; an example is the word *bat*. Bat has three phonemes: /b/, /a/, and /t/. Researchers at NICHD discovered that being able to read was based on the knowledge that words can be separated into phonemes. This process then becomes *phonemic awareness*. When your child has phonemic awareness she can begin to recognize that the written letters of the alphabet make up words.

You need to set up a meeting with the teacher as soon as possible and see what the school is doing to assist your child with reading intervention strategies. Does the teacher know that you have hired an outside tutor to help? You may also want to bring the tutor along and set up a plan of action to help your child.

Reading is a process, and it is a good thing that this teacher is on top of it. There is a lot that can be done to improve your child's reading skills, and she may be able to be promoted to second grade if you and the school take action. It is extremely important that you participate in the school's efforts to assist your child. After your initial meeting, meet or talk to your child's teacher on a weekly basis to see how she is progressing. Also set up a formal meeting four weeks before the second early literacy test in May for a final strategy session between the teacher, the tutor, and yourself.

Meanwhile, you can do things at home to help your child. The following exhibit, adapted from a National Institute for Literacy brochure, provides simple tips for parents to help their children read.

Put Reading First: Helping Your Child Learn to Read: Preschool Through Grade 3

Success in school starts with reading.

When children become good readers in the early grades, they are more likely to become better learners throughout their school years and beyond. Learning to read is hard work for children. Fortunately, research is now available that suggests how to give each child a good start in reading. Becoming a reader involves the development of important skills, including learning to:

- *Use* language in conversation.
- *Listen* and respond to stories read aloud.
- *Recognize* and name the letters of the alphabet.
- *Listen* to the sounds of spoken language.
- *Connect* sounds to letters to figure out the "code" of reading.
- *Read* often so that recognizing words becomes easy and automatic.
- *Learn* and *use* new words.
- *Understand* what is read.

Preschool and kindergarten teachers set the stage for your child to learn to read with some critical early skills. First-, second-, and third-grade teachers then take up the task of building the skills that children will use every day for the rest of their lives. As a parent, you can help by understanding what teachers are teaching and by asking questions about your child's progress and the classroom reading program.

You can also help your child become a reader. Learning to read takes practice, more practice than children get during the school day. Here is what a quality reading program should look like at school and how you can support that program through activities with your child.

If your child is just beginning to learn to read:

At school you should see teachers . . .

- *Teaching the sounds of language.* The teacher provides opportunities for children to practice with the sounds that make up words. Children learn to put sounds together to make words and to break words into their separate sounds.
- *Teaching the letters of the alphabet.* Teachers help children learn to recognize letter names and shapes.
- *Helping children learn and use new words.*
- *Reading to children every day.* Teachers read with expression and talk with children about what they are reading.

At home you can help by . . .

- *Practicing the sounds of language.* Read books with rhymes. Teach your child rhymes, short poems, and songs. Play simple word games: *How many words can you make up that sound like the word "bat"?*

Put Reading First: Helping Your Child Learn to Read: Preschool Through Grade 3, Cont'd.

- *Helping your child take spoken words apart and put them together.* Help your child separate the sounds in words, listen for beginning and ending sounds, and put separate sounds together.
- *Practicing the alphabet by pointing out letters wherever you see them and by reading alphabet books.*

If your child is just beginning to read:

At school you should see teachers . . .

- *Systematically teaching phonics—how sounds and letters are related.*
- *Giving children the opportunity to practice the letter-sound relationships they are learning.* Children have the chance to practice sounds and letters by reading easy books that use words with the letter-sound relationships they are learning.
- *Helping children write the letter-sound relationships they know by using them in words, sentences, messages, and their own stories.*
- *Showing children ways to think about and understand what they are reading.* The teacher asks children questions to show them how to think about the meaning of what they read.

At home you can help by . . .

- *Pointing out the letter-sound relationships your child is learning on labels, boxes, newspapers, magazines, and signs.*
- *Listening to your child read words and books from school.* Be patient and listen as your child practices. Let your child know you are proud of his reading.

If your child is reading:

At school you should see teachers . . .

- *Continuing to teach letter-sound relationships for children who need more practice.* On average, children need about two years of instruction in letter-sound relationships to become good spellers as well as readers.
- *Teaching the meaning of words, especially words that are important to understanding a book.*
- *Teaching ways to learn the meaning of new words.* Teachers cannot possibly teach students the meaning of every new word they see or read. Children should be taught how to use dictionaries to learn word meanings, how to use known words and word parts to figure out other words, and how to get clues about a word from the rest of the sentence.

Put Reading First: Helping Your Child Learn to Read: Preschool Through Grade 3, Cont'd.

- *Helping children understand what they are reading.* Good readers think as they read and they know whether what they are reading is making sense. Teachers help children to check their understanding. When children are having difficulty, teachers show them ways to figure out the meaning of what they are reading.

At home you can help your child by . . .

- *Rereading familiar books.* Children need practice in reading comfortably and with expression using books they know.
- *Building reading accuracy.* As your child is reading aloud, point out words he missed and help him read words correctly. If you stop to focus on a word, have your child reread the whole sentence to be sure he understands the meaning.
- *Building reading comprehension.* Talk with your child about what she is reading. Ask about new words. Talk about what happened in a story. Ask about the characters, places, and events that took place. Ask what new information she has learned from the book. Encourage her to read on her own.

Make reading a part of every day.

- *Share conversations with your child over mealtimes and other times you are together.* Children learn words more easily when they hear them spoken often. Introduce new and interesting words at every opportunity.
- *Read together every day.* Spend time talking about stories, pictures, and words.
- *Be your child's best advocate.* Keep informed about your child's progress in reading and ask the teacher about ways you can help.
- *Be a reader and a writer.* Children learn habits from the people around them.
- *Visit the library often.* Storytimes, computers, homework help, and other exciting activities await the entire family at the library.

Source: Adapted from a National Institute for Literacy RMC Research Corporation brochure, developed with funding from the National Institute for Literacy (ED-00-CO-0093). National Institute for Literacy, P.O. Box 1398, Jessup, MD 20794-1398; (800) 228-8813; or edpuborders@edpubs.org. See www.nifl.gov.

Test Talk! • Understanding the Stakes and Helping Your Children Do Their Best

Snapshot #44: My Child Failed Another Test

Whenever my child takes a test, he never looks it over first, but jumps right into it. He doesn't understand that if he knows what to expect on the test, he will be better prepared as he answers the questions. I've talked about this repeatedly with him, but no matter how hard I try, he just doesn't follow my advice. Consequently, his grades aren't as high as they should be. I know that he is a lot smarter than his test scores indicate. What should I do?

Tip: Sit your child down so you have his full attention. First, praise your child on how well he is doing in school and how proud you are of his effort. Then explain your ideas on how he can best tackle taking a test so that he performs his best. Sometimes if you talk about your own experiences taking tests when you were a student, your child will realize that your advice can work and will be more willing to listen. Emphasize again the importance of reading the questions first. Suggest that, if allowed, he circle the main points and key words on the actual test paper. Explain how this will help him as he moves through the test. If this doesn't work, ask for a conference with the teacher and your child, explaining why you want to meet so she will be prepared. She may even have more helpful tips for you and your child on test-taking. Always keep a log for your records on all communications with the school. (See Documentation Templates in Chapter Five.)

> *Knowing what to expect aids in preparation and concentration when tackling any problem.*

Snapshot #45: When a Test Is Over, Is It Really Over?

Once my child takes a test, he forgets about it completely. While I'm glad he doesn't stress over the test or his results, I feel he should look at the test and see what mistakes he made. I often ask to review a returned test with him, but he tunes me out. What should I do?

Tip: You're right to want to review every returned test with your child. Explain that this should be a regular part of his homework routine. Go over the portions he answered incorrectly and make sure he understands the concepts. If he tries to ignore you, mention that these questions and concepts will probably turn up on the year-end test. If he continues to tune you out, you may need to sit down with your child and develop an after-the-test contract.

After-the-Test Contract

Date: _____

I promise to review with my parent(s) the test results as soon as my teachers return them to me.

I will work on correcting the mistakes and highlighting the new information.

I will save these papers as studying tools for my next exam.

_____   _____
Child's Signature   Parent's Signature

After the Contract Is Signed

It is important to give feedback in a suitable time frame to let your child know how she is doing.

- Be specific—state those goals your child has achieved to increase your child's motivation to continue.
- Discuss any concerns you have.
- Listen and let your child have time to give her feedback on how the contract is going. If she's having difficulty meeting the terms of the contract, perhaps she needs more time, or the terms need to be redefined.
- Be prepared to make changes if necessary, and then come to new terms on which you both agree.

Snapshot #46: My Child Doesn't Do Well on Quizzes

My child is a good student. She can usually study at the last minute and do well on scheduled exams. However, when I looked over her Test Results Log (see Chapter Five), I noticed some of her grades ranked much lower than others. When I questioned her, she said her new teacher likes to give pop quizzes and she doesn't do well on them. My response was first one of surprise that the teacher would give so many pop quizzes and then disappointment that my child is not doing well on them. What should I do?

Tip: If your child is doing all of her studying at the last minute, she's not only going to do poorly on pop quizzes but probably will not retain as much information as she should. For a student to do her best work, she must be prepared for anything. Explain to your child that teachers test frequently for her own benefit. The more quizzes a teacher gives, the better prepared your daughter will be for big exams. She will cram less and know more. Also, the teacher's grading philosophy may be that scores on many little quizzes are equal to one big test score. Your child should understand that she can ruin her grade point average by not doing well on the quizzes. Her job is to study and review nightly, so when her teacher gives a surprise quiz she will be prepared and earn a good grade. You might also suggest to your daughter that she look ahead to the next chapter in the textbook so she is prepared for the next day's lesson—just in case the teacher decides to give a quiz at the end of the day.

> *Staying a step ahead is the way to travel the road to success.*

Snapshot #47: Help! My Child's Test Scores Are Back and I Don't Understand What They Mean

I received my child's results on the state standardized test, and frankly, I'm confused. It's difficult to tell whether my child did well or not. I am not sure what all the numbers mean. There is an explanation booklet attached to the results, but I am still confused. What should I do?

Tip: You are probably not the only parent who is feeling confused. Sometimes schools or the PTA will offer workshops for parents on how to interpret the test scores. If such a workshop does not exist, see whether the school staff can put one together or ask if someone can give you a simple explanation of what the scores mean. Talk to the teacher, guidance counselor, assistant principal, or principal, if necessary, to get help in interpreting your child's test scores. Don't let this drop! You need to understand the scoring so you can assist your child in knowing where any problems are and in learning strategies that will help improve future test scores.

> *Ask questions and know the meaning behind the score results.*

Snapshot #48: My Child Keeps Making the Same Types of Errors on His Tests

I save my child's test and school papers and I have noticed he keeps spelling the same words incorrectly and makes the same punctuation errors time after time. Sometimes he misses the whole point of a question. I wonder whether he didn't read the question thoroughly, didn't have enough time for the test, was so nervous he couldn't concentrate, or something else was going on I don't even have a clue about. He has all these state and district tests to take and if he is making mistakes on teacher-made tests now, I'm worried about how he will perform later on when it really counts. What should I do?

> *Understanding the test scores and being able to analyze test data can give you a picture of skills that have been learned and those that need to be retaught.*

Tip: You are definitely on the right track in analyzing your child's past tests and returned papers. This is exactly what principals and teachers are doing. You have done well to recognize the trends in his mistakes. Now is the time to develop a plan with the teacher that concentrates on those areas in which he is struggling.

Have your child bring home his textbooks. There are usually practice tests in the chapters that are being covered. The more he reviews, the more proficient he will become. Meet with the teacher and ask him whether he has any extra worksheets or ideas for you. Once you have made him aware of your child's weak areas, he will be able to assist him in class.

Topic: What to do with returned test papers
Problem: Your child is making mistakes on tests and class work even though he knows the material
Solution: Find your child's test traps

To find out whether your child is falling into any common test traps, ask him these questions.
   Are you:

- Cramming the night before?
- Spending too much time on one question instead of skipping it and coming back to it later?
- Spending too much time on a section and not finishing the test in the allotted time?
- Rushing through the test?
- Reading in a hurry and not realizing the questions may have more than one direction to follow?
- Not taking time to align the bubble answers to the right question?
- Not using a No. 2 pencil?
- Not making an outline for essay questions?
- Not answering essay questions fully?
- Not eliminating the most obviously incorrect answers on a multiple choice test?
- Forgetting to turn horizontal math problems into a vertical format so they are easier to compute? For example, are you changing

$$5 + 4 =$$

to

$$\begin{array}{r} 5 \\ + 4 \\ \hline \end{array}$$

- Forgetting to memorize important facts?
- Not visualizing a math word problem to figure out whether addition, subtraction, multiplication, or division is needed?
- Not looking carefully at all the labeled parts on a graph or map question to fully understand how to answer the question?
- Looking for shortcuts when there are none?
- Writing sloppily so the teacher can't read your responses to the essay questions or notes on the graphs and time lines?
- Not looking the complete test over to make sure you've answered all the questions?

Snapshot #49: I Save Every Test That Comes Home and I Am Running Out of Room

My child brings home all of her test papers every Friday from school. I put everything in a drawer and look them over after I receive the next report card to make sure that the grades match her papers. By the end of the year, I have boxes full of her tests and quizzes. I want to keep these so I can compare her grades from year to year and from semester to semester, but I am running out of room. I am not sure what I should keep after the school year is over. I can't keep everything. What should I do?

Keep only the necessities.

Tip: At the end of the year, go through all the test papers and pick out two or three samples of math, reading, writing, social studies, and science from each reporting period. Make sure there is a date, including the month and year. You want to keep samples that show exactly how your child performs. Separate the test papers by subject, put them in color-coded file folders, and label them by subject and grade. For example, you may choose red for math and blue for reading. Designate one folder to hold copies of all report cards, interim reports, conference sheets, and any other official school papers. Label each major folder by year. Now purchase a file cabinet or file box so you can clean up that clutter.

Snapshot #50: My Child Earns Good Grades in School But Scores Poorly on Standardized Tests

Every year I hear the same thing from my child's teacher: "Your son is so smart, but he tends to be lazy and sloppy when he takes his standardized tests." If he is so smart, why can't he get better grades on standardized tests? I'd like to change this trend. What should I do?

Tip: Schedule a parent-teacher conference and bring along your child's latest test scores as well as last year's test results. Let the teacher know that while you are pleased with your son's grades, you are worried about future standardized tests. Explain your concern that if he continues his pattern of poor testing, he might be retained. Make it clear you feel it's very important that his poor attitude toward testing change and you need her support. Suggest that a team approach might help your son demonstrate greater effort and become more focused, and ask her for any ideas or help she might be able to give. Next, have a talk with your son about the importance of testing well. Emphasize that testing is not just used in school, but also in real life, such as when people apply for a job. He needs to understand that good grades alone are not enough. In school and in the work world, he will often be judged by how well he performs on a test.

Make It Happen Test on "After the Test"

Let's see how good you are at taking tests. Review this chapter and take the following test on what you should be doing to help your child after the tests come home. You'll find the answers at the end of the book.

Directions: Circle either true or false to answer the following questions.

True	False	1.	Tests are given to young children because all children need practice on how to take a test.
True	False	2.	Cramming for a test produces the same results as studying well in advance.
True	False	3.	Your child should answer the hardest questions on a test first.
True	False	4.	Parents should be familiar with the skills and state standards for the grade level that their child is in.
True	False	5.	The main purpose for the No Child Left Behind Act was to determine which children will be retained at their present grade level.
True	False	6.	Your child should read a passage first and then answer the test questions.
True	False	7.	The more quizzes a teacher gives, the better prepared your child will be for big exams.
True	False	8.	Always save returned tests to use as a review.
True	False	9.	If a math problem is written horizontally, have your child figure it out in that format.
True	False	10.	It is important as a parent to understand all of the results of a standardized test.

Notes:

CHAPTER FIVE
The Academic Portfolio

> "No one who ever gave his best regretted it."
> **George Halas**

Testing provides a snapshot of your child's knowledge—his strengths and his weaknesses. Now that you understand the importance of testing and have learned how to view the results, you might wonder how you can take all of this information and use it for your child's benefit. The answer is: create an *academic portfolio* for your child. This portfolio will track your child's performance throughout his school history, giving you and your child's teachers a factual and invaluable look at "the total child."

In this chapter you will be given charts and templates to create a personalized portfolio for your child that tracks test scores, standardized testing reports, report card grades, and teacher conferences. As you gather information and other documentation, you will be creating an important tool to help your child achieve lifelong academic success.

What makes a good portfolio? What should be included? Why bother to keep a portfolio? Portfolios are important because they provide a more complete picture of a child's knowledge, skills, interests, and successful undertakings. Since the documentation it holds spans a period of time, a portfolio shows a child's development (or the lack thereof), which can help relieve uncertainty or reveal areas that need improvement.

Academic portfolios should include, but not be limited to, the following items:

- Tests
- Quizzes
- Surprise quizzes
- Standardized test results
- Group projects
- Individual research reports
- Journals and logs
- Interim reports
- Report cards
- Copy of conference reports

However, each school year is different. You need to keep appropriate records each year to help you, your child, and the school track your child's progress.

So what should you keep? As your child starts his first formal school experience in kindergarten, begin by keeping documentation that pertains to early literacy and prereading skills, report cards, teacher conference logs, any formal tests (such as an early literacy test and scores), and any other important information that you as a parent feel is crucial to create an academic snapshot of your child.

The early grades cement a solid educational foundation. Third grade is crucial—if your child is having reading difficulty, YOU must reach out to the school and get help. If help has not been provided for you, act fast—DO NOT WAIT! Reading is vital to your child's ability to succeed in school. Third grade is the first year that your child will be given the state assessment mandated under No Child Left Behind.

Early grades should keep the following documents:

1. Standardized test results
2. Report cards and any interim reports
3. Copies of conference reports

When your child moves on to middle school (grades 6 to 8) you will notice that the academic areas in which your child had difficulty in earlier grades—1 to 5—will become a big area of struggle if they were not remedied earlier. During the middle school years, it's important for you to keep special emphasis on teacher conferences, standardized tests, reading assessments, and special projects and analyze where your child's strengths and interests are. During these years many schools give students a career assessment test to determine what they want to do or be when they "grow up." Some schools provide academic career counseling at this early stage to begin to get students interested in careers that they may excel and have an interest in.

When your child enters high school this academic snapshot becomes a great blueprint for you and your child's school counselor. This documentation is crucial if you have moved to another state or district and want to make sure your child is placed in classes at the appropriate level. High school provides a repertoire of class choices: honors, advanced placement, regular, remedial. Some schools have college tracks, vocational tracks or intensive career programs, or both. You and your child need to choose what is best; using the academic portfolio will help you as you meet with your child and the school counselor.

In sum, keeping an academic portfolio as your child progresses from elementary to middle school to high school and beyond will assist you in seeing areas of strength and weakness. As your child goes through these educational milestones you can be ready to get him help, if help is needed, ensuring the best possible education for your child and peace of mind for you! In addition, having your child state and reach for yearly academic goals will keep him on track. These goal sheets become important when your child is struggling.

The following examples and templates will help you keep a complete record of your child's progress throughout his school years. We recommend that you keep this documentation in an accordion file, file box, or file cabinet for easy access. You can also find a sample portfolio at our Web site. Simply go to www.school-talk.com and you will be able to download templates you can personalize for your child.

Documentation Samples
Sample Communications Report Log

Date	Who Called the Conference	Who Was Present	Reason for Conference	Outcome	Follow-Up Date
Sept. 13	Parent	Parent, teacher	Child was put in lowest reading group.	Parent will review returned tests with child and work with him on missing skills. Ask teacher for helpful strategies.	10/15
Oct. 17	Teacher	Parent, teacher	Follow-up meeting on reading group.	Saw some improvement; stay in same group.	11/15

Sample Test Results Log (Partially Completed)

Directions: Here is a sample chart with the subject, date the test was given, and the grade received on the test. You may want to keep a similar log to keep track of your child's test progress in each subject. This sample log only shows grades through the second quarter, but you will want to keep the log all year. This will alert you to a subject that your child may need help with.

Subject	Sept.	Oct.	Nov.	Dec.	Jan.	Feb.	Mar.	Apr.	May	June
Math	79, 88, 75	66, 73								
Reading	A, A, B+	C, A								
Social studies	67, 69, 62	89, 97								
Science	98, 80	89, 93								
Writing	C, C	B, C								
Language arts	88, 89	87, 76								
Other	PE 90	PE 92								

Test Talk! • Understanding the Stakes and Helping Your Children Do Their Best

Sample Standardized Test Tracking Sheet

Grade	Date	Name of Test	Subject	Percentage
2	Feb. 06	SAT	Math	89%
2	Feb. 06	SAT	Reading	75%
3	Mar. 07	State Test	Math	85%
3	Mar. 07	State Test	Reading	71%

Sample Vision and Goals for School Success Sheet

Grade	Goals for Child This Academic Year	Goals for Future
3	Become a better reader, study every night.	Be on the honor roll.

Sample Conference Planning Form

Date	Problem	Goals	Teacher/Student Roles	Parent Roles
9/15/07	Homework	Hand in on time completed and accurate.	Put homework in the teacher's box first thing every morning. Teacher will remind child.	Make sure child puts homework, signed by parent, into backpack.
10/19/07	Tardy	Be to school on time.	Bell rings at 8:00 a.m. Positive reward when on time.	Prepare lunch/backpack night before. Leave house 10 minutes earlier.

Sample School Goals Chart

Goal	Monday	Tuesday	Wednesday	Thursday	Friday
1. Neat work	☺	☺	☺		
2. Homework handed in on time		☺		☺	
3. Projects completed		☺			
4. Met all project deadlines					
5. Accurate class work		☺	☺	☺	☺

Documentation Templates
Communications Report Log

Directions: Every time you meet with your child's teacher, bring the Communications Report Log with you. Keep this form at the front of your folder in order to track all your school communications, written or oral.

Date	Who Called the Conference	Who Was Present	Reason for Conference	Outcome	Follow-Up Date

Test Results Log

Subject	Sept.	Oct.	Nov.	Dec.	Jan.	Feb.	Mar.	Apr.	May	June

Standardized Test Tracking Sheet

Directions: Every year fill in the blank lines with the important data that the standardized test reported.

Grade	Date	Name of Test	Subject	Percentage

Vision and Goals for School Success Sheet

Grade	Goals for Child This Academic Year	Goals for Future

Conference Planning Form

Date	Problem	Goals	Teacher/Student Roles	Parent Roles

Test Talk! • Understanding the Stakes and Helping Your Children Do Their Best

School Goals Chart

Goal	Monday	Tuesday	Wednesday	Thursday	Friday

Whether you've read every page of *Test Talk!* or simply focused on those snapshots that address the needs of you and your child, we hope you found some great tips and strategies for test-taking. Because we want to be sure you understand the important part you play in your child's testing success, we recommend that you go back to the Introduction and retake the Test Communication Assessment and the Parent Homework Survey (toward the end of that chapter). You may also want to periodically review your responses to the Monthly Self-Evaluation (at the end of the Introduction). Ask yourself the following questions:

- Did any positive changes occur?
- Do I take notice of my child's successes and give praise?
- Are there still adjustments that I need to make as a parent to better assist my child?

If you are not happy with your answers, maybe you need to reread the parts of the book that pertain to your areas of concerns and try some of the tips again. Take the time to really analyze what is going on; it could simply be that you just weren't as consistent as you should have been while trying to make the necessary changes to your child's habits and attitudes. If you are still uncertain about your child's test-taking abilities and attitudes toward tests, you may want to approach the teacher or other school professionals for additional assistance.

> *Always take the time to review past experiences; this allows you to make changes to the present, which in turn lets you positively influence the future.*

Final Thoughts: Get Involved

Here's what you can do:

- Attend all planned parent-teacher conferences. There is usually one in the fall and one in the spring. Mark your calendar.

- Attend the school's Open House so you can meet your child's teacher and understand her homework and test policies. This is the first opportunity to find out about those important issues that can lead your child to school success.
- Become a member of the school's parent organization.
- Contribute to the fundraising efforts even if you don't need the item. If you buy just one thing, it can make a difference.
- Attend all special events at the school.
- When you find out about a class trip, offer to chaperone. If you work, plan ahead.
- Visit the school and school district's Web sites frequently.
- Take the time to read all flyers, notices, and newsletters.
- If you work and cannot physically be in the school during school hours, offer to take some of the teacher's projects home to work on them for the teacher. Any time you put in will be greatly appreciated by the staff.

> *Getting involved in the school shows your child that you care about his school and what goes on there. Your involvement can lead to your child taking his schoolwork more seriously.*

Make It Happen Test on "The Academic Portfolio"

Let's see how good you are at taking tests. Review this chapter and take the following test on how to put together a complete academic portfolio. You'll find the answers at the end of the book.

Directions: Read each question carefully and fill in the blanks.

1. Testing provides a snapshot of your child's _____ and _____.

2. What do test scores reveal? _____
   _____

3. Why are academic portfolios important? _____
   _____

4. What should be included in an academic portfolio? _____
   _____

Notes:

APPENDIX A
Glossary of Testing Terms

Academic portfolio A portfolio offers a way to assess a student's cumulative growth and progress through multiple samples of work. The difference between a portfolio and an exam is that the portfolio provides numerous examples of a student's progress and illustrates how that child has progressed over time. A portfolio might contain all science tests, lab reports, and projects completed in a given period of time. It might include only written documents, or could be more inclusive by containing artwork, photographs of projects completed, or recordings of oral work. Some colleges have gone to portfolio assessment to determine admission of students and subsequent placement into classes.

Achievement test Achievement tests are one example of standardized tests that measure the amount of knowledge a child has acquired in any given subject area compared to a large, national group of his peers. Some examples of well-known achievement tests are the Iowa Tests of Basic Skills, the Stanford Achievement Tests, the California Achievement Tests, and the Stanford-Binet Intelligence Scale.

Aptitude test An aptitude test might seem very much like an achievement test, but it measures something altogether different: a child's potential for future academic success. The most commonly known examples of these are the SAT and the ACT, frequently used to determine college admission.

Assessment *Assessment* is a general term used to define any means of evaluating progress, standing, or achievement. It can refer to a range of evaluative processes—from informal feedback from questionnaires, oral discussions, or unit tests that might occur in the individual classroom to scores from the district, state, or national standardized testing.

Bell curve A bell curve is a numerical, statistical device designed to test the validity of a test. Assuming that there is no such thing as "grade inflation," then only those students who truly demonstrate excellent command of content knowledge should receive an A on a test. Statistically, this would be a small number. The majority of students would receive a C on a test—demonstrating adequate command of the knowledge. Approximately the same number of students who earned A's and B's would also earn D's and F's. Graphed onto paper, the results would show the largest proportion of students in the middle, with smaller groups at either end, creating a kind of visually bell-shaped curve.

Criterion referencing This term is often used in connection with some form of standardized testing. When criterion-referenced scoring is utilized, the maker of the test has determined what would be an acceptable proficiency level for a student at that age. All scoring is then done in relation to that particular level. For instance, on a criterion-referenced test, a child might be identified as knowing 20 percent more content matter or demonstrating several grade levels more competency than would be expected.

Dot tests A slang term sometimes used by younger children to refer to the tests where they have to fill in the "dot" with a No. 2 pencil.

Essay test An essay test (not an "S.A." test, as one unknowing student referred to it) is a kind of performance test that demands a student compose and write an answer to a question, based on stored knowledge and comprehension of the overall subject. This kind of test is often difficult for students because there is little information provided by the teacher, and the student must rely completely on acquired knowledge to generate the answer. To present an answer that demonstrates mastery of content, a child must be able to organize material, create coherent paragraphs, have good spelling and grammar, and easily handwrite the information. Although many educators feel this is a far better assessment of knowledge than a multiple choice or true-false test, where a student might guess a correct answer, this method is also more difficult for a teacher to grade, takes more time to administer, and requires some in-depth teaching of topic matter.

Evaluation A generic term for assessments, *evaluation* generally implies a judgment, meaning that a grade or a score will be attached.

Grade equivalent This type of score labels the performance of a student by grade and month. The first number indicates the grade level and the number after the decimal is the school month. For example, 3.8 translates to third grade–eighth month, 9.1 equals ninth grade–first month, 2.0 would mean second grade–beginning of school, and so on. Most educators use this score to represent the grade level at which a child is performing. If a child is in second grade getting ready to move up and has a grade equivalent in reading of 1.9, that would mean the child is a year behind; if the grade equivalent read 3.9, it would indicate the child is reading a year ahead.

High-stakes test When the results of an assessment have important consequences—such as admission into a college, whether a student can move up to the next grade level, the evaluation of a teacher, or the funding for a particular program—then the test is referred to as a *high-stakes test*.

Matching test An exam that provides two lists: one of questions and one of answers. The student must match the proper answer to the proper question. Frequently, this technique is used for definitions and concept testing.

Multiple choice test An exam that provides students with options to choose from when answering any question. A good multiple choice exam will be consistent in form, with each question having the same number of options. These can be a valid assessment of a student's understanding of content, provided the answers are probable and clearly worded.

NAEP National Assessment of Educational Progress, commonly referred to as NAEP, is the organization that has been recording and monitoring the performance of American students in basic subjects for the longest period of time. Because of its longtime standing and continuing history, this group is accepted as a reliable source of information among both educators and policymakers.

National percentile rank Shows the standing of a student in comparison to other students across the nation in the same grade (the norm reference) who took the test at a similar time. Scores go from 1 percent (very low) to a high of 99 percent. Scoring at the fiftieth percentile would usually indicate average performance; scoring at the twenty-second percentile would mean the child is in the upper echelon, above seventy-eight of one hundred peers.

National stanine These scores, which range from a low of 1 to a high of 9, offer a comparison. (The term *stanine* is short for *standard nine-point scale*.) Stanine scores of 7, 8, and 9 indicate above-average performance; stanine scores of 4, 5, and 6 are average; and stanine scores of 1, 2, and 3 indicate below-average performance.

Norm referencing Norm referencing is the type of scoring used on standardized tests. When a score is norm-referenced, it means a child is being assessed with regard to where he places compared to a nationwide group of his peers (the norm group). (See "national percentile rank.")

Performance test This kind of test requires the student to perform a task or take an action to demonstrate command of subject matter. A performance test does not allow for preselected answers, as a multiple choice test does, where an answer can be guessed correctly. Instead, a child taking a performance exam might be asked to play a song on the recorder to prove her ability to read music. Other kinds of performance exams include conducting a science experiment, working out a mathematical problem on the board, or writing an essay. Performance tests require original responses, but they can be difficult for a teacher to grade. They are also time-consuming and can be costly to administer.

Raw score Number of questions answered correctly out of the total amount possible.

Short answer Short answer tests fall into the realm of essay-question and performance-based testing because they require the student to draw on his acquired knowledge. The short answer is generally a response that can be given in a few lines instead of the longer, multiple-paragraph answer required in an essay exam.

Standard error of measurement A term referring to the "leeway" given on the validity of test scores. For example, a child receives a score of 81 in math on a test that has a standard error of measurement of 3. Statistically, that child might score as low as a 78 or as high as an 84 on the same test if it were retaken.

Standardized test A standardized test is any exam that has predetermined performance levels and is administered and scored in the same way for all who take it. Standardized tests measure a student's standing relative to a peer group.

Standards Standards are predetermined descriptions of levels of content mastery or performance expected of a child at a certain age and grade.

Test bias For the standardized tests to be valid and to accurately assess a student's standing, questions must be included that could be correctly answered only by a small percentage of students—often students with educational advantages and higher economic standing. Critics of such testing suggest that the need for these questions creates an unfair bias against students from lower economic groups. This situation is referred to as *test bias*.

APPENDIX B
Resources and References

Government

National Dissemination Center for Children with Disabilities (NICHCY). Web site: nichcy@aed.org
P.O. Box 1492
Washington, DC 20013
(800) 695-0285
(202) 884-8441 (fax)

National organization that provides information on disabilities; IDEA, which is the special education law; NCLB; children with disabilities; and effective educational practices.

National Institute of Child Health and Human Development (NICHD)
P.O. Box 3006, Rockville, MD 20847
(800) 370-2943
(888) 320-6942 (TTY)
(301) 984-1473 (fax)
NICHDInformationResourceCenter@mail.nih.gov

Provides information on health issues.

National Institute for Literacy
1775 I Street N.W., Suite 730
Washington, DC 20006-2401
(202) 233-2025
(202) 233-2050 (fax)

Provides information and serves as a resource for literacy programs.

No Child Left Behind (NCLB).
Web site: www.NCLB.org
U.S. Department of Education
400 Maryland Avenue S.W.
Washington, DC 20202
(800) USA-LEARN
http://www.ed.gov/

Provides funding opportunities, student financial assistance, and research and statistics for educational organizations, professional educators, parents, and students.

Office of English Language Acquisition
U.S. Department of Education
400 Maryland Avenue S.W.
Washington, DC 20202
(800) USA-LEARN
http://www.ed.gov/offices/OELA/

Provides limited English–proficient students with equal access to equal educational opportunities.

Institute of Education Sciences
U.S. Department of Education
400 Maryland Avenue S.W.
Washington, DC 20202
(800) USA-LEARN
http://www.ed.gov/about/offices/list/ies/index.html?src=mr

Expands knowledge of and provides information on the condition of education, practices that improve academic achievement, and the effectiveness of federal and other education programs.

National Center for Education Statistics
1990 K Street N.W.
Washington, DC 20006
(202) 502-7300
http://nces.ed.gov/

Collects and analyzes data related to education both in the United States and abroad.

Common Core of Data
1990 K Street N.W.
Washington, DC 20006
(202) 502-7300
http://nces.ed.gov/ccd/

Provides a comprehensive, annually updated, national statistical database of all public elementary ERIC (Educational Resources Information Clearinghouse) and secondary schools and school districts, whose data are designed to be comparable across all states.

National Library of Education
U.S. Department of Education
400 Maryland Avenue S.W.
Washington, DC 20202
(800) 424-1616
http://www.ed.gov/NLE/

Provides programs and activities in the Department of Education, publications and materials for other federal agencies, services and resources through ERIC, and statistics through the National Center for Education Statistics.

Educational Resources Information Clearinghouse (ERIC)
ERIC Project
c/o Computer Sciences Corporation
4483-A Forbes Boulevard
Lanham, MD 20706
(800) LET-ERIC
http://www.eric.ed.gov/

A nationwide educational information network.

Office of Elementary and Secondary Education
U.S. Department of Education
400 Maryland Avenue S.W.
Washington, DC 20202
(800) USA-LEARN
http://www.ed.gov/about/offices/list/oese/index.html?src=mr

Provides useful and timely information to enhance knowledge of elementary and secondary education programs and issues.

Office of Special Education Programs and Rehabilitative Services
U.S. Department of Education
400 Maryland Avenue S.W.
Washington, DC 20202
(800) USA-LEARN
http://www.ed.gov/about/offices/list/osers/index.html?src=mr

Supports programs that assist in educating children with special needs, provides for the rehabilitation of youth and adults with disabilities, and supports research to improve the lives of individuals with disabilities.

Testing

The College Board
45 Columbus Avenue
New York, NY 10023-6992
(212) 713-8000
http://www.collegeboard.com/

Connects students to colleges and opportunities by creating SAT and advanced placement programs.

Educational Testing Service
Rosedale Road
Princeton, NJ 08541
(609) 921-9000
http://www.ets.org/

Provides educational testing and measurement standards through educational research.

National Assessment Governing Board
800 North Capitol Street N.W., Suite 825
Washington, DC 20002
(202) 357-6938
http://www.nagb.org/

Sets policies for the National Assessment of Educational Progress (NAEP), commonly known as the "The Nation's Report Card."

National Center for Fair and Open Testing
342 Broadway
Cambridge, MA 02139
(617) 864-4810
http://www.fairtest.org/

Works to end the abuses, misuses, and flaws in standardized testing and to ensure that the evaluation of students and workers is fair, open, and educationally sound.

National Assessment of Educational Progress (NAEP)
Assessment Division, 8th Floor
1990 K Street N.W.
Washington, DC 20006
(202) 502-7400
http://nces.ed.gov/nationsreportcard/

Assesses American students' knowledge in various subject areas, including reading, mathematics, science, and writing.

State Departments of Education

Alabama Department of Education
P.O. Box 302101
Montgomery, AL 36104
(334) 242-9700
http://www.alsde.edu/

Alaska Department of Education and Early Development
801 West 10 Street, Suite 200
Juneau, AK 99801
(907) 465-2800
http://www.educ.state.ak.us/

Arizona Department of Education
1535 West Jefferson Street
Phoenix, AZ 85007
(800) 352-4558
http://www.ade.state.az.us/

Arkansas Department of Education
4 Capitol Mall
Little Rock, AR 72201
(501) 682-4475
http://arkedu.state.ar.us/

California Department of Education
1430 N Street
Sacramento, CA 95814
(916) 319-0800
http://cde.ca.gov/

Colorado Department of Education
201 East Colfax Avenue
Denver, CO 80203-1799
(303) 866-6600
http://www.cde.state.co.us

Connecticut State Department of Education
165 Capitol Avenue
Hartford, CT 06145
(860) 713-6548
http://www.state.ct.us/sde/

Delaware Department of Education
John G. Townsend Building
401 Federal Street, Suite #2
Dover, DE 19901-3639
(302) 739-4601
http://www.doe.state.de.us/

Florida Department of Education
Turlington Building, Suite 1514
Tallahassee, FL 19901-3639
(850) 245-0505
http://www.fldoe.state.de.us/

Georgia Department of Education
2054 Twin Towers East
Atlanta, GA 30334
(404) 656-2800
http://www.doe.k12.ga.us/

Hawaii Department of Education
P.O. Box 2360
Honolulu, HI 96804
(808) 586-3230
http://doe.k12.hi.us/

Idaho State Department of Education
P.O. Box 83720
Boise, ID 83720-0027
(208) 332-6800
http://www.sde.state.id.us/

Illinois State Board of Education
100 N. First Street
Springfield, IL 62777
(866) 262-6663
http://www.isbe.state.il.us/

Indiana Department of Education
State House, Room 229
Indianapolis, IN 46204-2798
(317) 232-6610
http://doe.state.in.us/

Iowa Department of Education
Grimes State Office Building
Des Moines, IA 50319-0146
(515) 281-5294
http://www.state.ia.us/educate/

Kansas State Department of Education
120 S.E. Tenth Avenue
Topeka, KS 66612-1182
(785) 296-3201
http://www.ksbe.state.ks.us/

Kentucky State Department of Education
500 Mero Street
Frankfort, KY 40601
(502) 564-4770
http://www.kde.state.ky.us/

Louisiana Department of Education
P.O. Box 94064
Baton Rouge, LA 70804-9064
(877) 453-2721
http://www.doe.state.la.us/

Maine Department of Education
23 State House Station
Augusta, ME 04333
(207) 624-6600
http://www.state.me.us/education/

Maryland State Department of Education
200 West Baltimore Street
Baltimore, MD 21201
(410) 767-0600
http://www.msde.state.md.us/

Massachusetts Department of Education
350 Main Street
Malden, MA 02148-5023
(781) 338-3000
http://www.doe.mass.edu/

Michigan Department of Education
P.O. Box 30009
Lansing, MI 48909
(517) 373-3324
http://www.michigan.gov/mde

Minnesota Department of Children, Families, and Learning
1500 Highway 36 West
Roseville, MN 55113-4266
(651) 582-8200
http://education.state.mn.us/mde/index.html

Mississippi Department of Education
P.O. Box 771
Jackson, MS 39205
(601) 359-3513
http://www.mde.k12.ms.us/

Missouri Department of Elementary and Secondary Education
P.O. Box 480
Jefferson City, MO 65102
(573) 751-4212
http://www.dese.state.mo.us/

Montana Office of Public Instruction
P.O. Box 202501
Helena, MT 59620-2501
(888) 231-9393,
(406) 444-3095
http:// www.opi.state.mt.us

Nebraska Department of Education
P.O. Box 94987
Lincoln, NE 68509
(402) 471-2295
http://www.nde.state.ne.us/

Nevada Department of Education
700 East Fifth Street
Carson City, NV 89701
(775) 687-9200
http://www.doe.nv.gov/contact.html

New Hampshire Department of Education
101 Pleasant Street
Concord, NH 03301-3860
(603) 271-3494
http://www.ed.state.nh.us/education/contactus.htm/

New Jersey Department of Education
P.O. Box 500
Trenton, NJ 08625
(609) 292-4469
http://www.state.nj.us/education/

New Mexico Public Education Department
300 Don Gaspar
Santa Fe, NM 87501-2786
(505) 827-5800
http://sde.state.nm.us/

New York State Education Department
Education Building
Albany, NY 12234
(518) 474-3852
http://www.nysed.gov

North Carolina—Public Schools
301 N. Wilmington Street
Raleigh, NC 27607
(919) 807-3300
http://www.dpi.state.nc.us/

North Dakota Education Department
600 E. Boulevard Avenue
Department 201, Floors 9, 10, and 11
Bismarck, ND 58505-0440
(701) 328-2260
http://www.dpi.state.nd.us/

Ohio Department of Education
25 S. Front Street
Columbus, OH 43215-4183
(877) 644-6338
http://www.ode.state.oh.us/

Oklahoma State Department of Education
2500 North Lincoln Boulevard
Oklahoma City, OK 73105-4599
(405) 521-3301
http://sde.state.ok.us

Oregon Department of Education
255 Capitol Street N.E.
Salem, OR 97310-0203
(503) 378-3569
http://www.ode.state.or.us

Pennsylvania Department of Education
333 Market Street
Harrisburg, PA 17126
(717) 783-6788
http://www.pde.psu.edu/

Rhode Island Department of Elementary &
Secondary Education
255 Westminster Street
Providence, RI 02903
(401) 222-4600
http://www.ridoe.net/

South Carolina Department of Education
1429 Senate Street
Columbia, SC 29201
(803) 734-8500
http://www.sde.state.sc.us/

South Dakota Department of Education and
Cultural Affairs
700 Governors Drive
Pierre, SD 57501-2291
(605) 773-3134
http://doe.sd.gov/

Tennessee Department of Education
Andrew Johnson Tower, 6th Floor
Nashville, TN 37243-0375
(615) 741-2731
http://www.state.tn.us/education/

Texas Education Agency
William B. Travis Building
1701 N. Congress Avenue
Austin, TX 78701-1494
(512) 463-9734
http://www.tea.state.tx.us/sboe/

Utah State Office of Education (USOE)
250 East 500 South
Salt Lake City, UT 84111
(801) 538-7500
http://www.usoe.k12.ut.us/

Vermont Department of Education
120 State Street
Montpelier, VT 05620-2501
(802) 828-3135
http://www.state.vt.us/educ/

Virginia Department of Education
P.O. Box 2120
Richmond, VA 23218
(800) 292-3820
http://www.pen.k12.va.us/

Washington Office of Superintendent of Public Instruction
Old Capitol Building
P.O. Box 47200
Olympia, WA 98504-7200
(360) 725-6000
http://www.k12.wa.us/

West Virginia Department of Education
1900 Kanawha Boulevard East
Charleston, WV 25305
(304) 558-0304
http://wvde.state.wv.us/

Wisconsin Department of Public Instruction
P.O. Box 7841
Madison, WI 53707-7841
(800) 441-4563
http://www.dpi.state.wi.us/

Wyoming Department of Education
Hathaway Building
2300 Capitol Avenue
Cheyenne, WY 82002-0050
(307) 777-7675
http://www.k12.wy.us/

ANSWER KEY

Chapter One: Why Test?

1. Achievement tests are based on standards. Standards let the school team know what your child has learned for his particular grade level and what needs to be worked on.
2. Three reasons are:
   a. Review chapter materials.
   b. Utilize critical thinking skills.
   c. Learn how to study.
3. Practice tests build confidence in test-taking skills and help students recognize what they know and what they need assistance with.
4. Testing highlights what skills a child has acquired and what she still needs to learn. Because of NCLB, there is more accountability required by schools and school districts; therefore, teachers tend to give more tests.
5. Timed tests set a time limit in which a certain number of questions must be answered. This helps a child practice for standardized tests, future college exams, and aptitude tests.

Chapter Two: Savvy Study Skills

1. A week.
2. Word association, visualization, rhymes, acronyms.
3. Test schedule calendar.
4. Easy ones first, more difficult ones last.
5. Key words and concepts.

Chapter Three: No Test Stress!

1. Scan the entire test before starting; find out how much time is allowed for the entire test; find out how much each question is worth; read directions and questions carefully; answer easiest questions first; check paper when finished.
2. The state's Web site, the teacher, school newsletters.
3. Make sure there are no scoring errors; correct mistakes; ask teacher for assistance if still not sure how or why the answer is incorrect; save all returned papers for future reference.

4. Read directions carefully; outline all information in the margin; write essay using facts only; be neat, do not erase—cross out unwanted statements with a single line; watch clock to make sure there's enough time left to check answers.
5. You need to know whether test results will account for grade level retention or promotion, whether the test measures knowledge gained or affects report card grades.

Chapter Four: After the Test

1. True. Practice gives confidence and teaches techniques for a variety of tests.
2. False. Have your child start to study at least a week ahead of the test and review class notes every night.
3. False. Your child should always answer the easiest questions first and then go to the ones she is unsure about.
4. True. Parents should be familiar with the skills and state standards for their child's grade level.
5. False. The main purpose for the No Child Left Behind Act was to determine how well schools meet a child's academic success.
6. False. Do just the reverse. Read the questions first and then underline or circle key words or concepts as he reads the passage.
7. True. The more quizzes a teacher gives, the better prepared your child will be for big exams.
8. True. Returned tests are an excellent way to review, but first have your child write in the correct responses to any questions that were answered incorrectly.
9. False. Always have your child rewrite the problem into a vertical format on scratch paper if he is not allowed to write in the test booklet.
10. True. It is important as a parent to understand all of the results of a standardized test.

Chapter Five: The Academic Portfolio

1. Strengths and weaknesses.
2. Whether your child is making learning gains.
3. They provide a more complete picture of a child's knowledge, skills, interests, and successful undertakings.
4. Academic portfolios should include, but are not limited to, the following items: tests, quizzes, group projects, individual research reports, surprise quizzes, journals and logs, report cards, interim reports, copies of conference reports, and standardized test results (state and district).

About the Authors

About Cheli Cerra

For more than twenty years, Cheli Cerra has helped thousands of children achieve school and life success. As a school principal and a mother of two, Cheli knows firsthand the issues that teachers, parents, and children face. She was the founding principal of one of the first K–8 schools in Miami–Dade County, Florida, Everglades Elementary. This school of fifteen hundred students received an A+ rating for two consecutive years under her leadership.

Cheli is the founder of Eduville, Inc., a company that provides resources and strategies for parents and teachers to help their children. Among these resources are *Smarter Kid Secrets*, a free monthly e-zine, and the http://www.eduville.com Web site, which is full of tips, techniques, and strategies useful for anyone interested in helping a child succeed.

Recognized as "The Right Choice" by *Women's Day Magazine*, and featured on over thirty radio shows throughout the country, Cheli is committed to helping teachers and parents come together for the success of children. Her seminars, coaching programs, and presentations have provided strategies that empower her audiences to action. She will captivate you by teaching the lessons learned from her in-the-trenches experience in public education. As both a wife and a working mother, she understands the realities of everyday life and creates strategies to meet these challenges quickly and easily. Her powerful message of immigrating to this country, learning the language, and adapting to a new culture, also give Cheli a unique insight to the real-world challenges children face today.

Co-creator of the School-Talk Success Series: *Teacher Talk!, Parent Talk!, School Board Talk!, Principal Talk!,* and *Homework Talk!* For more information, go to http://www.school-talk.com.

About Dr. Ruth Jacoby

"Dr. Ruth" is the founding principal of the Somerset Academy charter schools, which include four charter schools with twenty-two hundred students in pre-kindergarten through twelfth grade. She has more than thirty years' experience as an administrator and educator in traditional public, private, and charter schools. Under her leadership, Somerset Academy became one of the first charter schools to receive SACS (Southern Association of Colleges and Schools) accreditation.

Dr. Ruth received her Ed.D. degree in child and youth studies for children from birth through eighteen years from Nova Southeastern University. She received her master of science in special needs and bachelor of science in early childhood and elementary education from Brooklyn College.

During the past three years, Dr. Ruth has become actively involved in educating other charter school personnel in how to develop standards-based curriculum and assessments. Her school was one of the founding partners of the Tri-County Charter School Partnership, which has implemented three South Florida Annenberg Challenge grants in student assessment and school accountability and three Florida Charter School Dissemination Grants. She serves on several governing boards for charter schools in Miami–Dade County, Florida, and is an active member of the Florida Consortium of Charter Schools. She has also taught as an adjunct professor on various colleges campuses and has written graduate courses.

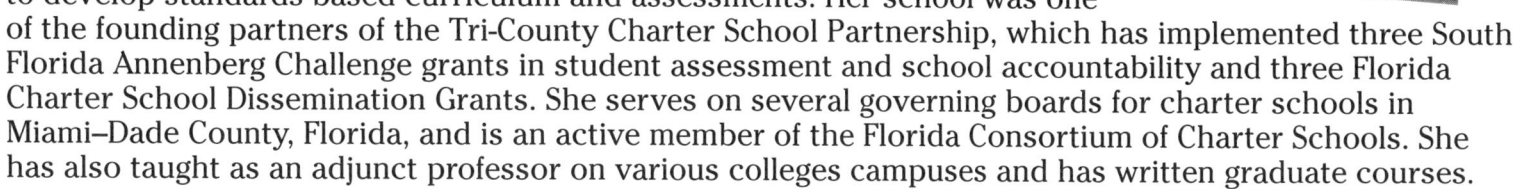

Co-creator of the School-Talk Success Series: *Teacher Talk!*, *Parent Talk!*, *School Board Talk!*, *Principal Talk!*, and *Homework Talk!* For more information, go to http://www.school-talk.com.

A Very Special Thanks To:

Our husbands: Tom Cerra and Marty Jacoby, for their unconditional love
Our children: Alexandra, Frank, Sari, and Scott, for their patience
Our Wiley editors: Kate Bradford and Connie Santisteban
All of the teachers, students, parents,
and community leaders
who have touched our lives
Our wonderful staff, colleagues,
and outstanding schools
And you, our reader, for reading,
absorbing, learning, sharing,
and growing

"Effective communicators always leave a piece of wisdom with their audience."

To your artful and effective communication.

Cheli and Ruth

Let us hear from you . . . send us your snapshots. E-mail Cheli and Ruth at:

Cheli Cerra
Cheli@school-talk.com

Ruth Jacoby
DrRuth@school-talk.com

Other Books by Cheli Cerra and Ruth Jacoby

Teacher Talk!: The Art of Effective Communication

208 pages/Paper   ISBN: 0-471-72014-3   www.josseybass.com

A must-have book for every practicing and would-be teacher!

Teacher Talk! provides fifty-two "snapshots" of typical situations that teachers in kindergarten through high school might encounter. It gives clear suggestions and tips for handling each situation that all involve simple ways to communicate with the child and/or the parents. Tips are organized by grade level, and often include several suggestions if the first ones don't work. The book is arranged by month to follow the school calendar and includes helpful checklists, worksheets, tracking sheets, and sample letters—all set up to give teachers the tools they need to work through specific situations and organize their thoughts and other information.

- Are you uncomfortable speaking with parents?
- Are you in need of assistance at conference time?
- Are you looking for easy-to-use worksheets and sample letters to guide you?
- Are you in need of answers on how to best handle common, everyday situations?

If you answered yes, then *Teacher Talk!* is the book you need. You'll communicate better with students and parents, your stress levels will go down, and student achievement will go up!

"An amazing compilation of what to say to parents. Any one suggestion will help, if not save your life, in a difficult situation with a parent. This book is a must for your professional library!"

—Harry K. Wong, Ed.D. Author of the #1 bestseller *The First Days of School*

Parent Talk!: The Art of Communication with the School and Your Child

128 pages/Paper   ISBN: 0-471-73303-2   www.josseybass.com

From "My teacher is picking on me!" to "I don't understand the results from my child's standardized test," this must-have guide provides fifty-two "snapshots" of typical situations that parents of school-age children might encounter, and offers clear, simple suggestions for positive resolutions. *Parent Talk!* features parent-to-parent tips and role-playing activities where parents can practice what to say when issues arise. The helpful checklists, worksheets, and progress reports make this book a wonderful resource for any parent.

Organized by season, the snapshots guide parents through the academic year, addressing just about every conceivable situation that can arise between a parent, a student, and a school.

Principal Talk!: The Art of Effective Communication in Successful School Leadership

144 pages/Paper   ISBN: 0-7879-7911-2   www.josseybass.com

"*Principal Talk! provides simple communication strategies and advice to keep teachers, students, parents, staff, and the community in your corner. A must-read for today's educational leader to be successful in today's reform climate.*"

—Jack Canfield, co-author, *Chicken Soup for the Teacher's Soul* and *Chicken Soup for the Parent's Soul*

A must-have book for all principals!

Principal Talk! offers principals and assistant principals of grades K–12 a down-to-earth resource for refining their communication skills. Organized month-by-month, the book's fifty-two practical and useful scenarios to implement communication with teachers, parents, students, staff, and the community follow with the academic year. Keep your cool and soar to new heights with insightful tips, worksheets, checklists, and sample letters for leadership success. For aspiring as well as veteran principals, this no-nonsense book summarizes how to be an educational leader and an advocate in today's educational environment.

Other Books by Cheli Cerra and Ruth Jacoby

**School Board Talk!:
The Art of Effective
Communication**

144 pages/Paper   ISBN: 0-7879-7912-0   www.josseybass.com

For both the aspiring and the veteran school board members, this book offers tips, worksheets, and practical advice to help board members develop and improve communication skills, survive in political office, and make a difference in education. In its user-friendly, easy-to-browse pages, you'll find fifty "snapshots" and solution strategies on topics such as casting the lone "no" vote and surviving, keeping your family in your fan club, building a school board team, handling constituent calls, and conquering the e-mail and memo mountain.

"Before taking office and periodically thereafter, all board members should read and re-read this book! This will make you a better board member while demonstrating to everyone you understand the role of the board and that of the superintendent and staff. It will also assist you in succeeding in one of the most critical and complex, but satisfying elected public offices."
—G. Holmes Braddock, Former President of the Council of Great City Schools and a thrity-eight-year veteran school board member, Miami–Dade County Public Schools

**Homework Talk!:
The Art of Effective Communication
About Your Child's Homework**

160 pages/Paper   ISBN: 0-7879-8273-3   www.josseybass.com

Put an end to nightly homework battles!

Homework Talk! provides parents with simple and practical advice to help them deal with the many issues that can come up surrounding their children's homework. Cheli Cerra and Ruth Jacoby have identified fifty-two typical homework situations and provided tips, strategies, and advice for handling each of them. *Homework Talk!* provides suggestions for handling each situation, from the child who forgets assignments to the teacher who's not responding to your questions, offering simple ways to communicate with the child, the teacher, and the school. The book contains checklists, worksheets, and progress reports to help work through specific problems and organize information.

Are you concerned about:

- Making sure your child is doing all of his homework on time?
- Talking to a teacher who assigns too much homework?
- Understanding how much help to give your child?
- Motivating your child to handle homework issues on her own?
- Overcoming your child's resistance to doing particular types of homework?

If you answered yes to any of these questions, then *Homework Talk!* is the book you need. Don't wait to start working with your child and your child's teachers to make homework a simple and productive process for everyone.